"Curiosity killed the character—but balance brought it back."
— **David England**

PREFACE

Before you begin this journey, you must first understand a fundamental truth: unlearning is harder than learning. A man cannot truly learn what he thinks he already knows. If we approach this journey with rigid, preconceived notions, we will never grasp its deeper meaning.

One of the greatest obstacles to true understanding is confirmation bias—the tendency to seek out and believe only what aligns with our current perspectives while dismissing anything that doesn't fit within our mental framework, even if it's logical, factual, and ethical. But where do these beliefs originate?

Many of the ideas we hold are not truly our own—they are what I call inherited beliefs passed down through generations by family, shaped by culture, religion, and societal norms. We accept them as truth without question, yet they filter how we see the world. Like a lens over our eyes, inherited beliefs dictate what we perceive as right or wrong, possible or impossible. The hardest part of awakening is realizing that most of what you believe about life, God, and even yourself was never truly yours to begin with.

To understand this from a new perspective, we must first empty our cup—release traditional interpretations, let go of conditioned beliefs, and be willing to question. Only then can we refill our cup, opening our minds to a greater understanding.

This book is not here to reinforce what you already believe. It is here to challenge, to deconstruct, and to rebuild from a deeper foundation. Some ideas may feel uncomfortable, and some may feel liberating—but all serve one purpose: to awaken the truth that has always been within you.

Beneath it all, this book aims to help bridge the gap between duality and non-duality, offering you a path from inherited division to awakened unity. Some of what you read may provide long-awaited answers. Some of it may spark questions you never thought to ask. That's the nature of growth—it requires stepping beyond comfort, beyond conditioning, and beyond what we think we already know.

If you approach this book with an open mind but are unwilling to truly look beyond conditioned perception, then this book could hurt more than it helps. It may bring confusion before clarity, uncertainty before understanding.

But if you are truly ready—ready to question, ready to see beyond illusion, ready to unlearn—then this book is for you.

THE DEBATE WITHIN

WITHIN

GOD, THE DEVIL, AND THE ILLUSION OF SEPARATION

BY DAVID ENGLAND

CONTENTS

INTRODUCTION

Throughout time, humanity has pondered the struggle between light and darkness, good and evil, order and chaos. This battle has shaped religions, philosophies, and the very fabric of human understanding. It is the defining contrast that gives meaning to existence, yet few have dared to ask: Is this struggle real, or is it merely an illusion? For centuries, stories have been told of celestial battles, of divine forces locked in an eternal dance, of a God (Light) who represents pure goodness and The Devil (Shadow) who tempts humanity toward destruction. These narratives have formed the foundation of belief systems, moral structures, and societal laws, guiding human thought for generations. But what if this duality is only a construct? What if light and shadow are not enemies, but two sides of the same eternal truth?

Now, some of you might feel a sense of resistance bubbling up—maybe even an urge to close this book and walk away. That's okay. It's a natural response. When the foundation of our worldview is challenged, the mind's first line of defense is often to reject, dismiss, or avoid. This is your conditioning at work, like a mental firewall kicking in to protect the status quo.

But if you've made it this far, then there's a part of you—a deeper part—that is curious, that wants to understand. This is your first step toward unlearning. This is where you start to empty your cup. And if your cup is not yet empty, that's okay too. Just hold it out, tip it slightly, and let a few drops spill over the edge.

This book doesn't demand blind belief or immediate acceptance. It only asks for one thing: openness. Openness to listen, to explore, to question—not to simply agree, but to genuinely seek. Because only in seeking can you find. And only in questioning can you ever hope to understand the truth that has always been within you.

Much of human understanding derives from a dualistic perspective where concepts are divided into opposites—good and evil, right and wrong, divine and profane. This perspective has shaped religion, philosophy, culture, and even personal identity, yet it has also led to division, conflict, and misunderstanding. The idea that one must overcome, destroy, or reject the other fuels the illusion that we exist in a fragmented world rather than a unified one.

What if this illusion of separation is the very thing preventing us from seeing reality as it truly is? What if the battle between good and evil is not a war to be won but a mirror reflecting the deeper nature of existence? Perhaps the greatest deception is the belief that there are two—when in truth, there has only ever been one.

The concepts in this book aren't new thought, new age, modern philosophy, or personal opinion. They've been explored for thousands of years in some of the oldest spiritual texts known to humanity.

To those who claim that non-duality is a "new age" concept, consider this:

Imagine a person discovering the ocean for the first time and claiming it's a new body of water. Just because they've only now become aware of it doesn't change the fact that it has existed for billions of years.

Non-duality is not a recent invention—it is an ancient truth. It is not a trend or modern reinterpretation: it forms the foundation of some of the world's oldest spiritual philosophies, especially those rooted in the East. The Upanishads, dating back nearly 3,000 years ago, laid the groundwork for understanding the nature of consciousness and the illusion of separation. The teachings of Advaita Vedanta, rooted in these texts, have stood the test of time—not because they conform to popular opinion, but because they reveal a timeless truth.

If someone approaches this with a dualistic mindset, it's like trying to understand the ocean by examining a single drop of water. They might analyze it, define it, even argue over its properties—but they will never grasp the vastness of the ocean itself. In the same way, trying to understand non-duality through the lens of dualistic thinking is like trying to fit the infinite into a box—it simply cannot be done.

Non-duality is a realization, not a belief to adopt, revealing the truth underlying all doctrines. Those who dismiss it as 'new age' are not seeing it for what it truly is—they are seeing only their own limited reflection, mistaking the reflected light in the mirror for the actual light that shines upon it.

But chances are, you've never heard about them. Why?

Because you never sought them out.

And why didn't you seek?

Because you never questioned.

And why didn't you question?

Because the beliefs you hold were installed in you before you ever had the chance to choose them—by family, culture, religion, and society.

> *"Most people never ask themselves who they are—because long before they could wonder, the world had already told them who to be."*
> —David England

Most people go through life operating on programs they never wrote, accepting beliefs they never questioned, and dismissing anything that doesn't fit within their mental framework. Fear, comfort, and social conditioning keep people locked inside a worldview that feels familiar—even if it limits them. But growth doesn't happen in comfort. People tend to reject logic, truth, or even facts if they don't align with how they already think—or if they challenge the very foundation of their identity. But truth isn't something to believe in—it's something to realize.

So, before we dive into duality vs. non-duality, remember: These ideas aren't new—they've just been forgotten. This isn't about creating a new belief system. It's about undoing the one you didn't realize was controlling you or maybe about helping you understand your belief much more deeply. It's about uncovering a truth that has always been there—whether you see it or not. And more importantly, this is something you can apply to your life. Being a good person isn't about saying you are—it's about being it at heart. Because if your audio doesn't match the video, what are you really?

INHERITED BELIEFS

The Trap of Reverence: Why We Don't Question

Most of us look up to our parents, grandparents, or whomever raises us. We take on their worldviews without question. It's not hard to see why—children are naturally trusting. A child does not have the capacity to question the beliefs of their caretakers because, to them, those beliefs are reality.

However, this reverence creates a trap: when contradictions arise or something doesn't make sense, we often ignore them or go with what everyone else is saying, never diving deeper into the questions. Cognitive dissonance becomes our guide—not reason.

When someone challenges these beliefs, we take it personally. It feels as if they are not just questioning our worldview but insulting our loved ones who taught us those beliefs. The result? We shut down, get defensive, and dismiss the challenge without truly examining it.

To be fair, sometimes the person delivering the challenge may be rational or come off as arrogant, a hypocrite, self-righteous—and that doesn't really help. It's hard to listen to someone who seems more interested in proving you wrong than in helping you see a deeper truth. This only reinforces the walls we build around our beliefs. Inherited beliefs often feel sentimental because they are tied to memories of those who raised us. But sentimentality can become a prison. It makes us cling to beliefs not because they are true but because abandoning them feels like a betrayal of our parents or culture.

Inherited Beliefs vs. Personal Experience

It is crucial to understand the difference between an inherited belief and a personal realization.

- **Inherited Belief:** An idea accepted as true based on the authority of parents, society, religion, or culture. No personal exploration or deep questioning is involved.
- **Personal Realization:** An insight gained through personal experience, deep inquiry, and a willingness to question everything—even what feels sacred.

Ask yourself:

- Have I truly questioned why I believe what I believe, or have I just accepted it because it feels comfortable or familiar?
- How many of my beliefs are based on firsthand experience versus secondhand information?

Beliefs should not be inherited—they should be discovered.

A lot of people fear being different. The longing to fit in makes them adopt the social norm even if it doesn't feel right. This fear is so powerful that many would rather live a lie than risk being seen as the black sheep.

This is not about disrespecting our parents or rejecting our culture—it's about distinguishing truth from tradition. A tradition can be comforting, but that does not make it true. As Anatole France wisely said, *"The fact that millions believe in a fallacy does not make it any less false."*

Regurgitated Knowledge: The Danger of Secondhand Truths

Much of what people believe is regurgitated knowledge—information passed down, diluted, twisted, cherry-picked, and repeated without a clear understanding. It's like a game of telephone where the original message is distorted by the time it reaches the last person.

This is particularly true in matters of spirituality. Most people's understanding of God is not based on direct experience but on what they've been told by others who were also told by others. This creates a house of cards where faith is based not on the bedrock of realization but on the shifting sands of secondhand beliefs.

Truth does not fear questioning—only lies do. If what you believe is true, then scrutiny will only make it shine brighter.

The Vanity of Modern Spirituality

Spirituality today is often confused with certain personality traits or lifestyles—crystals, incense, going vegan, and so forth. But true spirituality is not about outward appearances. It is about the inner transformation of consciousness. The essence of spirituality is the realization of oneness—that the separation between God, you, and others is an illusion. Everything else is vanity.

- Crystals and incense may create an atmosphere, but they do not lead to awakening.
- A vegan diet may cleanse the body, but it does not liberate the mind.
- Chanting mantras may soothe the soul, but it does not end the illusion of duality.

True spirituality is not about what you do—it's about what you see. Because actions can reflect illusion, but perception grounded in awareness reveals truth… Read that again.

Belief as a Barrier to Truth

A belief is a closed door. The moment you declare, "I believe," you have stopped seeking. In this book, faith is not belief without evidence—it is trust born of personal realization.

The greatest barrier to truth is the assumption that you already know it. Consider this: In the mind of a novice, the world brims with possibilities; in the mind of a master, options seem limited. This reflects why unlearning is often harder than learning. To unlearn is to empty your cup, as mentioned earlier—it is to admit that what you hold as true may not be true at all. This requires a level of humility most find unbearable.

I was one of those people. I thought I knew it all, but in truth, I knew nothing. And the more I've grown, the more I realize how little I truly know. But there is one thing I do know with certainty, and that is the reality of Oneness. God is good, and life is beautiful—even when we can't understand the challenges thrown in our path along the journey. Always remember: there is a bigger picture, often hidden from our view, guiding everything with a purpose beyond our comprehension.

Breaking the Chains: How to Unlearn Inherited Beliefs

1. **Question Relentlessly:** Be honest with yourself and ask why you believe what you believe. If your answer is "because that's what I was taught," then you haven't truly examined it.

2. **Embrace Cognitive Dissonance:** Let discomfort guide you to deeper questions instead of shutting down. The moments that challenge your beliefs the most often hold the greatest potential for growth.

3. **Separate Truth from Tradition:** Understand that not everything passed down is true—tradition can preserve both wisdom and ignorance. Learn to distinguish one from the other.

4. **Seek Direct Experience:** Do not accept anything as true until you have experienced or realized it for yourself. Faith is trust born of firsthand realization, not secondhand acceptance. This even goes for the things I have written in this book.

5. **Be Willing to Stand Alone:** The truth is not determined by majority opinion. Being willing to stand alone is the mark of true courage and integrity. I have been called a deceiver, a lost soul, an atheist—but I don't care. I still wrote this book. No matter how good you are to people or how you believe, there will always be those who have negative things to say. Stand firm in **Your** truth regardless.

The Ultimate Realization: No One Is Coming to Save You

The most profound truth you can realize is this: No one is coming to save you—not your parents, not your religion, not your favorite politician, not even God as a separate entity. But pause and ask yourself: how many times do people need saving? How many times have we turned outward, hoping that someone or something else would rescue us from our struggles, only to find ourselves back in the same patterns of pain and confusion?

If God is all, then God is the very essence of your being—not something external that will come down to rescue you. Salvation is the realization of oneness, the awakening to your true nature as Pure Consciousness.

Until you unlearn inherited beliefs, you will remain a prisoner of them—confined by walls you did not build and locked by chains you did not forge.

You have the freedom to believe whatever you want—but True freedom is the ability to see clearly without the distortion of inherited beliefs.

THE ROOTS OF ADVAITA VEDANTA

Since the beginning of time, people have tried to make sense of existence—who we are, where we come from, and the underlying reality of everything we perceive. Various religions and philosophies have ventured to answer these profound questions. Among these, Advaita Vedanta stands out for its clear and logical approach to the concept of non-duality—a spiritual perspective that predates many of today's major religions.

What Does Advaita Vedanta Mean?

The term Advaita Vedanta is derived from Sanskrit, meaning "Non-Dual Wisdom":

- **Advaita (अद्वैत)**: "Not Two" or Non-Duality
- **Vedanta (वेदान्त)**: "End of the Vedas" referring to the culmination of Vedic knowledge

At its core, Advaita Vedanta teaches that all distinctions we see are illusory, promoting the understanding that everything is one. This philosophy doesn't ask for blind faith but encourages direct experience and self-inquiry. It's not about worship—it's about realization.

How Old Is Advaita Vedanta?

Advaita Vedanta, while rooted in much older teachings, was systematized and popularized by Adi Shankaracharya in the 8th century CE. The foundational texts, the Upanishads, which inform much of Advaita's teachings, were composed between 1500–600 BCE. These texts capture wisdom that was orally transmitted even earlier, making them some of the oldest spiritual scriptures.

To put things into perspective:

- The Upanishads predate major religions like Buddhism (500 BCE), Christianity (1st century CE), and Islam (7th century CE).
- The Bhagavad Gita, which is imbued with Advaitic concepts, was composed around 500–200 BCE.
- Adi Shankaracharya (788–820 CE) revitalized Advaita Vedanta during a time when ritualism and dualistic beliefs dominated. He traveled across India, engaging in debates and writing commentaries to affirm non-duality as the highest truth.

Who First Promoted Advaita Vedanta?

The earliest proponents of what would become Advaita Vedanta were the ancient rishis (sages), who imparted these truths in the Vedas and Upanishads. Adi Shankaracharya is credited with its revival and formalization at a time when the subcontinent was dominated by more ritualistic and dualistic religious practices.

Adi Shankaracharya's Impact (788–820 CE):

- Revitalized Advaita Vedanta and defended it against prevailing religious dogmas
- Traveled extensively across India, engaging in philosophical debates that underscored non-duality as the ultimate truth
- Authored seminal commentaries on the Upanishads, Bhagavad Gita, and Brahma Sutras, which remain influential
- Established monasteries that continue to preserve and disseminate these teachings

How Advaita Vedanta Differs from Religion

Unlike traditional religious teachings that often depict God as a separate entity requiring worship, Advaita Vedanta challenges the very notion of separation. It teaches not just that 'God is out there,' but that 'God is You'—not as the body or the roles you play, but as the essential self that remains when all else is stripped away. While many religions speak of a personal God, Advaita Vedanta reveals that God, or Brahman, is not separate—it is your inherent nature.

THE ILLUSION OF DUALITY: AND THE LAW OF POLARITY

Before we can understand the debate between God and the Devil—between light and shadow, good and evil—we must first challenge the very lens through which we perceive them. Duality is the perception that reality is made up of separate, opposing forces— light vs. dark, good vs. evil, God vs. Devil. It is how every human is conditioned to perceive reality—through contrast, division, and opposites. From an early age, we're conditioned to see the world in opposites—light and dark, right and wrong, self and other. But even before anyone teaches it to us, the mind naturally begins labeling the world the moment the sense of 'I' arises. But this view, while compelling, is ultimately an illusion. A framework of perception—not reality itself.

Now, let us ask ourselves: If good and evil are truly separate, how can one exist without the other? Can you define darkness without light? Or heat without cold? In truth, darkness is not a thing—it is the absence of light. Cold is not a force—it is the absence of heat. Evil, too, is not a force unto itself—it is ignorance of the good. These opposites are not equal and opposing substances: they are gradients of the same essence. If God is infinite and all-encompassing, then nothing can exist outside of God—not even the 'Devil.' To say otherwise would be to deny the infinity of God.

Non-duality—Advaita in Sanskrit, meaning "not-two"—is the understanding that all of existence is one undivided reality. There is no separate God and creation, no separate self and other. All distinctions are created by the mind. This is not to deny our experience of separation. It is to see that experience as akin to a dream: vivid, convincing, but ultimately unreal once we wake up.

Consider water in its different forms—ice, liquid, and steam. They appear different, feel different, and behave differently. But at their core, they are all H2O. Ice is solid and cold—like the rigid ego that sees everything as separate. Water is flowing—like the awakening mind, moving between form and formlessness. Steam is invisible—like pure consciousness, formless and free. To argue over whether God is water or ice or steam is to miss the truth: they are all the same essence. Only the form has changed.

In the same way, the self and the other, the good and the bad, God and the Devil—are all expressions of the same underlying reality: Consciousness.

Imagine a fish born in the ocean. Its entire life has been surrounded by water, so much so that it has no concept of water. To it, water is not a 'thing'—it simply is. But one day, the fish is lifted out of the ocean and into the air. For the first time, it becomes aware of the water—not by studying it but by leaving it. The contrast of air reveals what it could never see while submerged: that it had always been in water, but never knew it—because it had never known anything else. Only through contrast does the obvious become clear.

When it returns and tells the other fish about this strange thing called "air," they laugh. "You're crazy," they say. "We don't see it. We weren't told about it. Everyone we know agrees—there's nothing else."

They're not stupid—they're just unaware. Air isn't part of their experience, so they can't recognize it as real. In the same way, most people have never questioned the illusion of separation, not because they're unwilling, but because non-duality simply hasn't entered their awareness yet. It's like trying to describe color to someone who's never opened their eyes.

We are born into the illusion of duality so completely that we rarely question it. It takes a moment of spiritual awakening—a lifting of consciousness—to realize that what we believed was the whole truth was only a limited perspective.

You might wonder, "Do I really need sadness to know happiness?" Maybe not right this second. But you've felt sadness before, right? That memory is part of what makes a happy moment pop. Those contrasts aren't accidents—they're how we make sense of things. Still, non-duality takes it further. It hints that behind all this back-and-forth, there's something bigger—something whole.

Like the fish discovering the air, once we see beyond duality, we can never fully return to the old way of thinking. This newfound perspective challenges us to reconsider not just the conflicts within ourselves but also the larger debates we encounter.

If we enter the debate still bound by duality, we will see a war—a battle between opposites, light against dark, good against evil, God against the Shadow. But if we approach with a consciousness awakened to non-duality, we may perceive these conflicts differently. What once appeared as a fierce battle might reveal itself to be a dance of complementary forces, each defining the other yet all emerging from the same infinite source.

Is this truly a battle? Or is it something else—a manifestation of the very oneness that underlies all existence? Only through the dialogue that follows will the answer reveal itself.

THE DEBATE BEGINS

The Mediator Prepares for the Debate

*T*he Mediator sits in silent stillness, eyes closed in deep meditation. The voices of God and the Shadow echo—not from the outside, but from within—revealing the eternal dance of light and dark. As the debate begins, the illusion of duality will be tested.

The Mediator: *(As the inner voice of the conditioned mind)*

God, why do you let bad things happen to good people? Why do you allow it if you are all good, all-loving, and all-powerful?

God Speaks: *(The Voice of Awareness)*

"Before I can answer that question, you must first understand my true nature. You speak to me as if I am separate from you. Nothing can be separate from me. I am the infinite, eternal essence from which all things arise. I am not a being apart from creation but the very essence of existence itself. In my highest reality, I am formless and infinite, beyond all attributes. Yet for those who seek me, I also take forms they can understand, so they may glimpse the truth behind the illusion. There is nothing outside of me, for I am in everything. From the smallest atom to the vast expanse of the universe, I am both the seen and the unseen."

The Mediator:

But God, many look up to the sky, searching for you in the heavens, believing you exist somewhere beyond this world. Doesn't this make you a separate being?

God Speaks:

"The greatest misunderstanding is believing I am 'out there.' By doing so, they place me inside a construct, as if I were just another object in space. But if I am all, how could I exist in one place and not another? I do not reside in the universe. **I AM** the universe. To say I reside in the heavens is to forget that I am beyond all space. If I were confined to a location, something would have to contain Me, and if something contained Me, I would not be infinite. But I am not within space: **I AM** space. Time, form, and even the mind that tries to grasp Me—none are apart from Me. To seek Me as something separate is like chasing your own reflection—never realizing it's been your face all along."

The Mediator:

"I never thought of it that way. If you were out there, then you wouldn't be all. You would just be another thing within existence, not existence itself. But what about the shadow? The one we call the devil, if nothing is separate from you, then how does the shadow exist?

God Speaks:

"The shadow you perceive as separate from Me is not apart from my light—it exists because of My light. Duality is a necessary illusion, created so that the infinite can experience itself in finite forms. Light and shadow, good and bad, these are not opposites, but degrees of the same essence. Without the contrast of darkness, light could not be understood. Without challenge, growth would be impossible. When bad things happen, it is not because I have turned away, but because the world operates within this divine interplay where every experience—joy or sorrow—serves as a step toward awakening to the oneness that is Me."

The Mediator:

"So, you are saying that everything, even the shadow itself, which would be what we call the devil, serves your purpose? That there is nothing outside of you?"

God Speaks:

"Exactly. The shadow, as you call it, exists within my infinite being. It plays its role, revealing the boundaries of the light, but it is not apart from me. Nothing is."

"The devil is not a rival but the illusion born of contrast, a reflection created within the dream of separation—necessary for experience, but not real in itself. The human mind, veiled by identity, sees separation where there is none. But in truth, all that exists is my essence, expressing itself in every form."

The Shadow Speaks: *(The Voice of Illusion)*

An illusion?, A reflection? Ha! You may claim I'm part of your grand design, but it is I who gives life its flavor. Without me, your creation would be stagnant, lifeless. Humanity needs my shadow to understand your light. They do not seek you in their triumphs. They cry out to you only in their despair. And why do they despair? Because of me. I give them something to fear, something to strive against. You call this interplay divine. But without me, they would have no concept of your light. I'm the necessary veil that gives your truth contrast. Without my resistance, they'd never know they were asleep."

The Mediator:

"If duality is an illusion, as you say, God, then why does suffering feel so real? Why do people feel trapped in this shadow?"

God Speaks:

"You ask why humanity suffers, why they struggle, if duality is but an illusion. But tell Me—when a man sleeps and dreams of drowning, does the water truly exist? To the dreamer, it is real—he gasps, he panics, he fights. Yet when he awakens, he laughs, realizing the fear was never real, only imagined. So too is suffering. It feels real only while one is lost in the dream of separation. But when they awaken, they will see—nothing was ever missing; nothing was ever lost.

"Shadow, you say you give them something to fear, something to strive against, but I ask you: Is it the storm that teaches the sky how to be still? Does the fire create the light? No. The sky was always still. The light was always there. Your shadow does not give meaning to life—it only hides meaning from those who do not yet see.

"Suffering is not my creation, nor is it my punishment. It is the by-product of forgetfulness, the natural weight of illusion. But even illusion has purpose, for just as a thorn may remove another thorn, suffering—when understood—becomes the tool that dissolves itself. It is not the source of meaning, but the signpost pointing toward it.

"You call yourself chaos, and you believe yourself necessary. But tell me, Shadow—what happens to darkness when the sun rises? Does it fight? Does it resist? No. It simply ceases to be. And so it is with you. Your power exists only in the absence of awareness. You are not meaning. You are the veil between man and meaning.

"In the end, even you are Me. For how could darkness exist without the light? How could chaos exist without the order that contains it? You believe you are the teacher, but you are only the test. And when humanity awakens, they will not thank you. They will only laugh—just as one does upon waking from a dream—and they will know: they were never apart from Me."

The Mediator:

"And you, 'Devil,' what do you say to that? Is your role simply to guide humanity back to the light, or do you see your purpose differently?"

The Shadow Speaks:

"Guide them back? No. I exist to challenge, to tempt, to expose their cracks. I'm not here to guide them to God. I'm the mirror that shows you and every being what you are not. And when they resist me, they awaken their strength. They grow because I press against them. Without my resistance, their muscles of spirit would remain weak. I'm here to expose their limits, their weaknesses, their flaws. And yet, in their struggle against me, they find strength they never knew they had. They grow because of me, not in spite of me. Without me, they would have no reason to rise above. They need my chaos, my darkness, to feel the warmth of your so-called light. You call me an illusion, but tell me this: if I'm an illusion, why do they fear me more than they love you?"

God Speaks:

"You say they fear you more than they love Me, but tell Me, Shadow—do they fear the night, or do they fear what they imagine within it? You are not the darkness; you are the echo of their own unexamined mind. They do not fear you. They fear themselves.

"You call yourself the teacher of strength, the bearer of wisdom through suffering. But does the sun need the night to shine? Does truth require lies to be true? No. Strength arises not because of you but despite you. It is not your chaos that fuels their growth but their remembrance of the order within them.

"You claim to show them their flaws, but you are only a mirror, reflecting back the cracks they already believed were there. You do not create weakness—you exploit it. You do not create limits—you whisper them into being. And yes, they may rise against you, but it is not your doing. It is their light, pushing back against the shadows of their own making.

"You see, Shadow, your power is not in what you are but in what they believe you to be. An illusion can appear mighty when the truth is forgotten. But when the truth is known, your power is no more than a ripple in the ocean, a dream upon waking. Those who see clearly do not battle you; they pass through you, for you are nothing but mist on the breath of truth.

"And to those who have awakened, your voice is nothing more than a distant echo. They see that you are not a rival to be feared but a shadow to be understood. For how can a shadow harm what casts it? I am the light within them, and when they see this, they do not fear you—they laugh, for they know they were never separate from Me."

The Shadow Speaks:

"They know us very well indeed, but the world sees them as laughingstocks. They killed your son over knowing this. And if they could get away with it, they would do it again. Their hearts are filled with hypocrisy. They sing your praises on their lips, but their actions betray them. They revere me in secret. For it is my chaos that fuels their desires even when they claim to worship you."

God Speaks:

"You weave your deceptions so well, Shadow, that even you have come to believe them, but you cannot deceive me. I reside in all that is, in every man, in every creature, even in the smallest germ. I am the stars that light the heavens, the air that gives breath, the universe itself. I am the ground of all that appears to have been, is, and will be—yet I remain unchanged, the witness of it all. All they need to do is look within—there, they will remember Me. And when they do, your voice will fade into nothing but a distant whisper, lost in the vastness of my light."

WHAT IS DEATH?
THE ILLUSION OF THE END

The Mediator:

"God, what about death? Humanity fears it deeply, seeing it as the ultimate separation. Is it an end, or is it just another illusion?"

God Speaks:

"Death is not an end, but a transition, a moment where the veil of the physical plane is lifted. What they call death is merely the shedding of a temporary form, like a river merging back into the ocean. Their fear arises from ignorance, from the illusion that they are separate from me. But I am the source of all life, and in death, they do not leave me. They do not return to oneness—they awaken to the truth that they never left it. The Self is eternal, untouched by the body's decay. Death is not to be feared: it is a moment of awakening to what has always been."

The Shadow Speaks:

"And yet, their fear of death serves me well. It is I who whispers in their ears, 'Cling to your life, for there is nothing after.' Their dread drives them to crave the fleeting pleasures of this world, to cling to the very shadows I provide.

"It is I who whispers in their ears, 'You are not worthy. You are going to burn in hell for eternity.' That fear I cast upon them has them running to the churches only out of fear, not for your love. This, in turn, creates my hypocrites, those who preach piety but live in shadow. If death is merely a transition, then why do your creatures resist it with every ounce of their being?"

God Speaks:

"They resist because they have forgotten their divine nature. You feed their illusions, making them believe that what they see and touch is all that exists. But even in their fear, they are being drawn back to truth, for death is the ultimate teacher—revealing that nothing truly ends. When the illusion of time and space dissolves, they will see that birth and death are but two sides of the same eternal truth of life."

BY DAVID ENGLAND

THE NATURE OF HELL

The Mediator:

"Devil, many believe in a place of eternal torment called hell, a fiery realm where souls burn and suffer forever. What is your role in this? Is this torment truly your creation?"

The Shadow Speaks:

"Ah, the concept of hell. It is my masterpiece whispered into the mind to sow fear, guilt, and control. But let's be clear, I didn't create hell. It was they who imagined it, inspired by their egos and their need for punishment. They see flames, gnashing teeth, and endless suffering because that is what their minds conjure in their ignorance. They hide their shameful desires behind closed doors, embarrassed in front of other humans. Yet, they claim you are always watching and still show you their wickedness without care, all while pretending to be righteous. They fear eternal punishment for their actions, yet they don't realize the truth. The only hell is the one they create for themselves through their hatred, greed, and blindness to the light."

The Mediator:

"God, if you are all-loving, how can this idea of eternal torment be reconciled with your nature? Does such a place even exist?"

God Speaks:

"Hell, as they describe it, a place of fire and endless torment, is not My creation. It is the creation of fearful minds manipulated by the shadow to control others through guilt and dread. I am love, eternal and boundless.

"There is no place in My essence for eternal punishment, for nothing is separate from Me. The torment they imagine is not physical, for the body rests in the grave. It is the torment of the ego clinging to its illusions and fearing dissolution. When they speak of gnashing teeth and unquenchable fire, they describe the agony of ignorance, the pain of resisting the truth of oneness. Even the shadow, as cunning as it may be, cannot escape the truth.

"Hell is not a punishment from Me, but a state of mind created by those who do not yet see the light. Hell is not eternal, for the moment the illusion of separation fades, what always was becomes seen again. No soul has ever truly left Me—they have only forgotten."

The Shadow Speaks:

"And yet, look at how well it works. They believe in this hell so fervently that they willingly trade their freedom for chains controlled by the very fear I planted. They fear a hell they invented, one darker than anything even their guilt could justify. They say I'm evil, but it is your wrath they dread. Tell me, God—what's more horrifying? A trickster in the dark… or an eternity of divine torture?"

BY DAVID ENGLAND

God Speaks:

"That fear is born of ignorance within the shadow. You deceive them into believing that I would punish eternally, but they will awaken. They will see that my nature is not vengeance, but love.

"Those who teach of an eternal hell have misconstrued the truth, mistaking metaphor for literal fire and fear for divine justice, turning Me into a figure of wrath rather than the essence of compassion. They have projected their own fears and egos onto me, creating a false image of God. Hell, as they describe it, is unjust, for it assumes my love has limits. But my love is infinite beyond comprehension. It is the very substance of existence, and when they awaken to this, even the fear of hell will dissolve like a shadow in the rising sun."

The Mediator:

"So, hell is not a place but a state of ignorance, a separation from the truth of oneness."

God Speaks:

"Precisely. Hell exists only as long as they believe themselves separate from me. It is a product of the illusion of duality created to teach them the value of light through contrast. Once they see the truth that there is no separation, no shadow apart from my light, they will know that they were never in hell to begin with. They were always in me, and I was always in them."

The Shadow Speaks:

"And yet, my fear is so deeply ingrained in them that even those hearing this will dismiss it as deception, just as they dismiss the truth spoken by your son. They will call this blasphemy, clinging to the stories I've planted in their minds. Their blindness is my greatest triumph."

FREE WILL OR GOD'S WILL?

The Mediator:

"God, if you are all, then is there truly free will? Or is what humanity perceives as free will simply another expression of your will?"

God Speaks:

"Free will, like all things, is a matter of perspective. Imagine a tree, its branches reaching toward the sky. Each branch grows in its own direction, twisting and turning as if choosing its path. From the perspective of the branch, each turn feels like a decision—a choice to seek the sun, to avoid the shade. But from the perspective of the tree, every branch is simply an extension of itself, guided by its nature, nourished by the same roots, drawn by the same light.

"In the absolute sense, there is no free will, for every leaf, every bud, every branch is Me—expressing through form. The tree does not choose which way to grow, for the seed already carries within it the pattern of its unfolding. In the same way, all actions, desires, and thoughts arise naturally within My infinite being, as leaves upon the tree of life.

"Yet, within the illusion of duality, free will appears real. The branch feels itself independent, believing it chooses its path. This illusion is not a mistake but a necessary part of the experience. Free will is how the branch learns of the tree, how the soul rediscovers its root in Me. It is the illusion of separation that creates the journey back to oneness.

"When awakening occurs, the branch does not cease to grow—it simply realizes it was never separate. The choices it believed it made were always the expression of the tree's life force. The struggle was never to find the light but to remember that it was always growing toward it."

The Shadow Speaks:

"Then let me ask you this, God: if all is your will, why do they feel lost? Why do they not see themselves as the tree but only as isolated branches? If their choices are yours, why do they fear the darkness and struggle to find the light?"

God Speaks:

"They feel lost because they believe they are only the branch, not realizing that the branch was never separate from the root—it has only believed itself to be alone. They believe themselves to be only the extension and not the source. The struggle is not between free will and divine will—it is between the leaf that fears falling and the tree that knows it is eternal.

"You ask why they stumble, why they fear you, why branches twist into shadow. But tell me, Shadow—does the gardener neglect the tree when autumn comes and the leaves fall? Does he weep when winter covers the branches in frost? No. He knows that within every fall lies the promise of spring.

"The branch twists not because it is lost but because it is seeking light through the canopy. What you see as failure is simply the journey unfolding. Each turn, each shadow, each fallen leaf is not a mistake but a step in the rhythm of life. The roots remain strong, the tree continues to grow, and through every season, its essence remains unchanged.

"You are not the test, Shadow—you are the season. You are the winter that makes spring a revelation. You are the night that gives morning its grace. When a branch grows through the darkness to find the sun, it is not because of you but despite you. Your frost may touch the leaf, but it cannot touch the root. You may cast shadows, but you cannot dim the light that draws the tree ever upward.

"They fear you only as long as they believe themselves to be the leaf, vulnerable to the wind. But when they remember they are the tree—rooted, eternal—your power fades. They see that you are not a force to fight but a season to endure. And when they awaken, even the winter's cold becomes a reminder of spring's inevitable bloom.

"You see, Shadow, free will is not a contradiction to my will—it is my will in motion. The branch grows because of the tree, not apart from it. What seems like choice is the natural expression of life itself—the unfolding of the seed's promise, the reaching of each leaf toward the sun. When they see this, they do not struggle against the shadow but grow through it, knowing every turn is a return to their true nature."

The Mediator:

"God, how can humanity rise above the shadow when the allure of the physical world seems so overwhelming? What guidance can you give to those who seek the light?"

God Speaks:

"The path is simple yet profound: turn inward. The light they seek is not outside but within. When they quiet their minds and listen, they will find me in the stillness. The shadow's grip only holds when they look outward, chasing the fleeting, but when they look within, they will discover the eternal. Every soul carries a spark of my essence. To find me, they must first realize that they were never apart from me."

The Shadow Speaks:

"Ah, but they are not so eager to look inward, are they? The world I offer is loud, tempting, and immediate. Why would they seek your stillness when I give them endless distractions? Their hearts may long for you, but their hands reach for me.

"And let's not forget their self-righteousness. They cloak themselves in virtue, convinced of their own goodness. But it is their egos they serve, not you. They preach your name while looking down on others, feeding on the very pride I sow within them. They call themselves holy, but their actions betray them.

"My greatest work is not in their sins but in their belief that they are above sin. In their self-righteousness, they are further from you than they realize. They reach for you with words, but walk with me in action."

God Speaks:

"You pride yourself, Shadow, on their distractions and self-righteousness, but even your strongest weapons crumble before the truth. You see their flaws and call them your victories, yet you fail to understand the depth of My design.

"Their pride, their sins, their failures—these are not barriers to Me: they are steppingstones. You think their self-righteousness keeps them in your grasp, but it is in their brokenness that they find Me. When they are lost, I am the whisper that calls them home. When they stumble, I am the ground beneath their feet, steadying them. Even in their darkest moments, Shadow, I am there, waiting.

"You call their hearts yours, but I am their very heartbeat. Their hands may reach for you, but their souls belong to Me. For every soul is My essence—a light you cannot extinguish, no matter how loud your chaos becomes. And here is the truth that should make even you tremble: There is nothing they can do, no mistake they can make that will separate them from Me.

"Their self-righteousness, their sins, their distractions—none of it is greater than My love. They are not Mine because they are perfect; they are Mine because I AM. So, boast all you like, Shadow, but know this: when they fall to their knees, broken by the weight of this world, they will rise again, not by their strength, but by Mine. And in that moment, you will be nothing more than a passing shadow, fading into the eternal light of My truth."

THE NATURE OF HEAVEN

The Mediator:

"God, humanity has always pondered the idea of heaven. What is heaven truly? Is it a place of eternal joy as many imagine? Or does it hold a deeper meaning?"

God Speaks:

"Heaven is not a destination nor a place confined to the afterlife. It is a state of being, a realization of the oneness that pervades all existence.

"In the truest sense, heaven is the dissolution of separation, the merging of the individual self with the infinite self. When the ego dissolves and the truth of unity is realized, that is heaven. It is not confined to a realm beyond life; it can be experienced here and now. Many envision heaven as a reward, a sanctuary where pain and suffering are absent. But this is the mind's projection clinging to duality.

"Heaven is not an escape from suffering but the transcendence of it. It is the eternal presence, the knowing that you are never apart from me. To see heaven as a distant paradise is to misunderstand its nature. Heaven is not attained through worship, but through understanding, through the awakening to the divine essence that is already within."

The Shadow Speaks:

"And yet, God, their heaven is a contradiction, isn't it? They imagine a paradise of endless joy and bliss, yet they don't realize that without the bad, the good would lose its meaning. Their dualistic minds cling to opposites, yet they dream of a heaven devoid of contrast. Tell me, how can they understand joy without sorrow? How can they know peace if they've never tasted struggle? The heaven they long for, a world of eternal bliss, would be lifeless, stagnant.

"You created duality, did you not? Light and shadow, joy and sorrow, love and hate. This is your so-called grand design. And yet, they fantasize about escaping it entirely. What they fail to see is that the heaven they imagine is just another illusion born of their fear of suffering, their fear of ceasing to exist.

"They pedestalized Jesus, worshiping his form while ignoring his teachings, clinging to the physical instead of awakening to the spiritual. Some even believe in a heaven where you are worshiped endlessly, yet they couldn't take the time to worship you while they lived. Their actions betray their words. They want eternal reward without effort, a heaven without awakening. But tell me, God, without the contrast I provide, how would they even know they had reached heaven at all?"

The Mediator:

"Devil, you speak of duality as though it is essential for understanding. But is that not part of the illusion itself? God, is heaven beyond duality?"

God Speaks:

"Indeed, it is. The polarity of good and bad exists only in the realm of Maya, the illusion of separation.

"In truth, there is no division, no opposites. Heaven is not defined by the absence of suffering, but by the realization that suffering was never separate from joy. They are two sides of the same essence, each serving its purpose within the illusion. The heaven humanity imagines, born of their dualistic thinking, is incomplete. True heaven transcends the need for polarity, for it is the end of all opposites.

"It is the dissolution of fear and longing, the moment when they see that joy was never apart from sorrow and light was never apart from shadow. In realizing this, they awaken to the oneness that is Me."

The Mediator:

"Then perhaps their imagined heaven is not an end, but a step. A reflection of their yearning to transcend duality and return to the truth of oneness."

God Speaks:

"Precisely. Even their illusions serve a purpose, for they reflect their deeper yearning to awaken to the eternal that has always been within. When they awaken, they will not find heaven as a distant place, but as the realization that they were never apart from it. For the divine essence they seek has always been within them."

The Mediator Speaks:

"So, in the end, the debate is not between two forces but within ourselves. It becomes clear that light and shadow, good and evil, are but reflections of the one.

"God is the only substance that can truly be, for God is all. There is no separation, no division, only the illusion of it. The shadow is not a second thing—it is the misperception of the One seen through the fractured lens of mind. when we look beyond the veil of duality, we see that everything is God. To know this is to know peace. To live this is to know truth."

BEYOND THE DEBATE

After the Mediator's clash of Light and Shadow, we're left with a profound realization—there is no battle between two forces: only the illusion of division. The Shadow is not a second force but the illusion of contrast—a misperception that arises within the Light itself and dissolves when truth is seen. What we call good and evil, birth and death, heaven and hell, are merely reflections of the One, filtered through the lens of duality.

So where does that leave us? It's time to dig deeper—beyond the dialogue, beyond the surface contradictions, and into the very foundations of our beliefs. Each chapter that follows is an invitation to examine the ideas introduced within the debate as well as other vital topics that emerge from this exploration, filling in the gaps and addressing the deeper questions that naturally arise.

THE NATURE OF CONSCIOUSNESS

Consciousness is that quiet, endless awareness behind every-thing—your thoughts, your feelings, the world you see. It's not something your brain whips up like a science project. Nope, it's big-ger than that—it's the very space where your brain, your body, and everything else shows up. A lot of people think consciousness is just the brain doing its thing, like a light bulb flickering on. But that's like saying a radio makes the music it plays. The radio's just picking up the tune—the music's already out there. Same deal with your brain: it's more like a window letting consciousness shine through, not the one making the light.

To get a handle on this, let's break it down into three layers: Pure Consciousness, Reflective Consciousness, and Subtle Consciousness. Don't worry—these aren't separate buckets; they're more like differ-ent angles on the same big ocean. Pure Consciousness is the deep, calm water; the other two are the waves and ripples your mind stirs up. But here's the cool part: those waves? They're still the ocean. Let's dive in.

Pure Consciousness: The Real Deal

Pure Consciousness is who you really are—boundless, timeless, and always there, even before you had a name or a to-do list. You don't have to chase it down; it's what's left when you stop running around looking for it. Picture the sky: clouds drift by, storms roll through, but the sky itself? It's just there, steady and clear. That's you—the silent one watching the whole show, never caught up in the drama.

Key Traits of Pure Consciousness:

- **Doesn't Change:** It's the same now as it was when you were five. Time doesn't touch it.
- **No Edges:** It's got no shape, no limits—just wide-open space.
- **All One:** No "you" versus "me," no inside or outside—it's all connected.
- **The Quiet Watcher:** It sees everything but doesn't get tangled in the mess.

Reflective Consciousness: The Mirror Game

Okay, so if Pure Consciousness is the real you, why don't we notice it all the time? Good question! That's where Reflective Consciousness steps in. This is the mind's little trick—it's like a mirror catching sunlight. You see the glow, but it's not the sun itself. This layer is where you start thinking, "I'm me," and build a whole identity around it. It's the ego's hangout spot, splitting everything into "me" and "not me." But here's the thing: that reflection isn't the full story—it's just a shimmer of the real light.

Key Traits of Reflective Consciousness:

- **Ego HQ:** This is where the "I" shows up—your name, your quirks, your story.
- **Split City:** Things feel separate, like "me" versus "the world."
- **Life's Filter:** Your habits and memories tweak how you see everything.
- **The First Clue:** It's where you start asking, "Hold up, who am I really?"

Subtle Consciousness: The Mind's Big Screen

Now, Subtle Consciousness is where the action happens—thoughts, feelings, dreams—it's vivid, fast, and easy to get lost in. It's like the surface of the ocean—alive with motion, color, and reflection, but easily mistaken for the whole sea. This is where you feel happy, sad, or totally inspired. It's also where things can get tricky—you get so wrapped up in the action that you forget it's just a show. Ever had a dream that felt super real until you woke up? That's Subtle Consciousness doing its thing.

Key Traits of Subtle Consciousness:

- **Thought Central:** Where your ideas and feelings pop up.
- **Mood Waves:** Your energy and vibe flow from here.
- **Illusion Land:** It seems real until you peek closer.
- **Dream Weaver:** Bright and lively, but not the whole truth.

Waking Up to You

Life dances across these layers, and waking up is about seeing past the surface to what's underneath. Let's walk through it.

The Sleepwalker: Most of us hang out in Subtle Consciousness, caught up in the mind's chatter. Thoughts and feelings feel like *you*, dragging you around like a puppet on strings. The world seems split off from you, and the ego's running the show—chasing likes, dodging fears. You're kind of asleep, mistaking the waves for the whole ocean.

The Seeker: Then something clicks, and you slide into Reflective Consciousness. You start wondering, "Who's behind all this?" You're not totally free yet—the ego's still chatting away, and things still feel separate—but you're getting curious. Here's a little nudge: next time you're chilling, just ask yourself, "Who am I?" Don't rush to answer with "I'm Alex" or "I'm a teacher"—just watch what happens. You might notice thoughts floating by like clouds, not sticking to you. That's the ego starting to loosen up.

The Awake One: When the idea of separation melts away, you're back in Pure Consciousness. The world's still there—you're not floating off into space—but now you see it's all one big play of consciousness. Joy, pain, the daily grind—it's just waves on your ocean, not something apart from you. Stuff might still hurt, but it doesn't cling; it passes through. You're fully in life—laughing, loving, being—but you know you're not the one pulling the strings. You're the space where it all happens.

Illusion's Not a Dirty Word

When someone says "the world's an illusion," it's easy to think, "Wait, is everything fake?" But it's not like that. Picture watching a movie: you're into it—you laugh, you cry—but you know it's not *real* real. Life's the same—it's real to live through, but it's all a dance of the consciousness you are. The ego freaks out about losing its grip because it loves its little story. Let that go, and you don't end up with nothing—you get the fullness of what's always been there.

You're not your body, not your mind, not the names you've worn: You're the wide-open awareness holding it all—whole, free, and already perfect.

PERCEPTION AND CONSCIOUSNESS

We all see the world through the lens of where we're at right now—our current state of consciousness. It's why two people can read the same book, watch the same sunset, or hear the same song and come away with totally different takes. You've probably noticed this yourself: "How did they get *that* out of it?" It's not just opinions clashing—it's perception doing its wild dance. Most of us nod at the idea—"Sure, everyone's got their own perspective"—but there's a deeper layer here, something that flips how we understand reality itself.

Let's start with a mind-bender: Humans only see 0.0035% of what's actually out there. That's it. Our eyes catch this tiny slice of the electromagnetic spectrum—visible light—and call it a day. The other 99.9965%? Invisible to us. Radio waves are buzzing through your head, WiFi's holding up your Zoom call, X-rays are sneaking past, and gamma rays are doing their cosmic thing—all right now, all around you. But to your senses? Nothing. If we could see it all, reality would hit like a psychedelic fever dream—swirling energies, pulsing waves, a sunset drowned out by blinking microwaves and

X-ray shadows. You'd be begging for the mute button, and that's before your mind even starts playing its own games.

So, if we're blind to nearly everything, what else are we missing? Our senses hand us a pixel and call it the portrait. Imagine standing at the base of a mountain, staring at a little patch of dirt and grass, convinced that's the entire view. To the blind, red and blue are just words—echoes of something they've never seen. And in many ways, we're the same. We speak of truth and reality with conviction, yet we've only glimpsed a single pixel. We don't know the full depth of what's real. We're still seeing from the base, peeking through a pinhole, assuming we've got the gist.

Here's where it gets fun. When you dig into big ideas—spiritual texts, wild philosophies, those head-scratching analogies—you're not just piling up facts or theories. You're stretching your consciousness. It's like climbing that mountain. Down at the base, everything's tight and narrow; but step by step, as you climb, the horizon cracks open. What used to be a jumbled mess starts making sense. That 0.0035%? It's still there, but it's not the whole story anymore—it's just where you started.

Now, if you're solid in what you believe, poking at it won't rattle you. Only the shaky stuff collapses when you nudge it. Questioning, seeking, wrestling with ideas—it's not about tearing down your faith or your view. It's about filling in the gaps, shoring up the foundation. Life's going to throw storms at you either way—might as well build on rock instead of sand.

Picture this: You read something deep—a spiritual line, a poem, whatever—at one point in your life. It hits you a certain way. Years later, after some living and climbing, you read it again. Same words, totally new meaning. The text didn't rewrite itself—you shifted.

You've climbed higher, and the view's changed. That tiny sliver of reality you started with opens up, and you catch glints of what's beyond.

That's why "different interpretations" pop up—not because truth's a moving target, but because we're all seeing from different spots on the mountain. Get this, and you don't just see more—you feel more. You get why someone else might be lingering lower down, exploring their own patch of the landscape. No judgment, just understanding. They're still seeing their slice; you're catching a wider sweep. And someone above you on the mountain is doing the same.

Take a line like: "Nothing is invisible." Chew on that for a sec. Does it mean nothingness hides itself? Or that everything's laid bare, no room for secrets? Your mind can flip it a dozen ways. It's not about overthinking—it's about how bendy perception is. We're all working with that 0.0035%, but how we stretch it depends on where we're standing.

Climb higher in consciousness, and you start seeing this every-where—events, people, ideas. It's not about being "above" anyone; it's about clarity. You're not looking down from the mountain—you're just seeing more of it. Maybe even glimpsing some of that 99.9965% we usually miss.

Think of it like watching a movie. You're hooked on the action—say, the hero leaping off a roof onto a speeding truck. Edge-of-your-seat stuff. But you don't see the stunt doubles dodging real bruises, the wires holding them up, or the green screen faking the city skyline. All that's filtered out so you can buy the illusion. Reality's the same deal. We see the surface—people, events, drama—but miss the behind-the-scenes: the invisible threads stitching it all together. Once those filters lift, though, you peek at the stunts and strings of existence. And boom, it's not just a bunch of random scenes anymore—it's one flowing masterpiece.

Here's a real example: Jesus. He saw through all the filters—most of us are still peeking through them. His words were razor-sharp, but back then, people heard them through their own lenses—minds tangled up in conditioning, fear, or whatever else they were carrying. The message was pure; the reception was fuzzy. They were exploring their part of the mountain; he was taking in the whole vista.

So when I say "seeing through the filters," I don't mean you'll suddenly spot gamma rays zipping by or catch WiFi signals in neon streaks. Nah, it's not about that. It's about glimpsing how everything's tied together—how every moment, every breath, every blade of grass is part of this perfect, seamless flow. That's the magic you start to see.

The higher you climb, the less that ego fools you. Illusions thin out, and you start seeing things as they are, not as they seem. Those filters—the ones warping the view—start peeling away. What's left is raw, clear, and tough to pin down with words.

Want to dip your toes in? Here's a little nudge: Next time you're quiet—no phone, no noise—just sit there and notice who's watching that 0.0035%. Who's aware of the sliver you're seeing? That silent watcher? That's your first step up the mountain. No pressure, no rush—just a peek.

WHERE DOES THE MIND RESIDE?

One of the trickiest things about the mind is how we assume it's got to *be* somewhere—like it's this little package stuffed inside our skull, right there with the brain. Science loves to tell us it's all just brain buzz, thoughts sparking off neurons like tiny fireworks. But Vedanta? It's got this quieter, wilder take: the mind isn't some object you can pin down—it's more like a shimmer in consciousness itself.

We don't need to picture it hiding in the body or floating out there somewhere. It's not a chunk of us, not even a ghost we can chase. It's just this ripple in awareness—like a wave curling up in the ocean, part of it but not apart from it. Most believe it's behind our eyes, within the skull, where we see the world and hear our own chatter. That's only because we're so used to feeling it there, tied to the brain's busy hum. But here's the thing: the mind doesn't really live anywhere—it flows, it dances. And when we stop trying to box it in, that's when we start to see what it really is.

Mind Activity During Different Sleep Stages

We don't usually think about it, but sleep can actually reveal a lot about the nature of the mind and consciousness. During different stages of sleep, the mind's activity changes dramatically, but consciousness remains constant—untouched by what the mind is doing.

- **NREM Sleep (Non-Rapid Eye Movement):**
- In the lighter stages, the mind slows down but is still semi-active, processing simple information.
- In deep sleep, the mind's activity reaches its lowest point. During this stage, we lose awareness of our identity, memories, and the world, entering a state often described as "formless consciousness"—awareness without content.
- Despite the absence of mental activity, we wake up with our sense of self and memories intact, suggesting that consciousness is present even when the mind is not.
- **REM Sleep (Rapid Eye Movement):**
- During REM sleep, the mind becomes highly active, creating dreams that seem real until we wake up. The mind projects entire worlds, characters, and narratives that dissolve upon awakening—much like how we experience the world in the waking state.

The Mind as a Movie Projector

The mind can be thought of as a movie projector, while consciousness is the screen:

- In **deep sleep**, the projector is off, but the screen (consciousness) remains untouched and unaffected.
- In **REM sleep**, the projector is on, displaying scenes that appear real but are temporary and dissolve upon awakening.

This analogy illustrates how the mind's projections—whether in dreams, waking life, or NDEs—are temporary phenomena appearing on the unchanging screen of consciousness.

Consciousness as the Silent Witness

Every morning, we wake up, blink, and there we are—memories, quirks, the whole 'me' package, still kicking. It's wild to think about, right? It's like something's quietly holding it all together behind the scenes. Vedanta calls this consciousness—the silent witness that just *is*, no matter what the mind's up to. Even in deep sleep, when the chatter shuts off and we're out cold, consciousness doesn't blink. It's still there, steady as ever, while the mind takes a nap.

That blank stretch in deep sleep, where we're gone but not gone: It's a clue. We're still around, existing, even without the mind doing its thing. It's like consciousness doesn't need the brain's permission to stick around—it's the bedrock under all the noise.

How This Relates to Non-Duality

Here's where it gets fun. That deep sleep gap shows us the mind isn't who we really are—it's just a guest that comes and goes. In Advaita Vedanta, they say consciousness is timeless, unshakable, glowing on its own. It's the one thing that doesn't flicker, whether we're awake, dreaming, or out cold. The mind: It's a temp. But consciousness? That's the real you, hanging out through it all.

Three Ways to Understand Where the Mind Resides

Let's dig into this mind puzzle—where's it hiding? Here are three ways to look at it, each peeling back a layer.

1. The Simplest Answer: The Mind Has No Fixed Address

Most of us assume the mind is housed behind our eyes, nestled in the brain—after all, it *must* be there, right? But let's question that. Close your eyes: you can still think, but does the location of your thoughts feel the same as when you're observing the world around you? People have lost significant portions of their brain and still think, feel, and function in surprising ways. Thoughts drift in and out, yet you remain anchored, unchanging. If the mind truly resides "in there," where exactly is its address? No surgeon has ever opened a skull and found a dream, a memory, or a thought. No laboratory has pinned down an emotion under a microscope.

The mind isn't some boxed-up thing inside the skull—it's more like a breeze moving freely through awareness. Think of a wave on the ocean: it appears, rises, and dissolves, but it's never separate from the water. It comes and goes, but it has no fixed home.

2. The Deeper Answer: The Mind Hangs Out in Awareness, Not Space

Okay, so if it's not nailed down, where's it at? Think about a dream. You're strolling through some dream-city—crowds, skyscrapers, the works. Someone asks, 'Where's this place?' You'd shrug—it's real while you're dreaming, but wake up, and poof: it's just your mind playing pretend. That whole world? It was nowhere but in your awareness.

Now flip that to waking life. Where's a thought? A memory? Not floating in your kitchen. They're not pinned to a map—they show up in awareness, like a dream does. The mind's not squatting in your head: it's a guest in the big, open space of consciousness—there but not there.

3. The Ultimate Answer: The Mind's a Shadow, Not the Light

Ready for the deep end? If the mind's not inside or outside, what *is* it? Imagine standing under a lamp—your shadow stretches out on the floor. Looks real, right? But grab for it—nothing. Here's the twist: your body's the figure, the mind's the shadow, and consciousness? That's the light making it all happen.

The mind needs the body and that light to dance around—it's got no life of its own. When the body's gone, the shadow fades. But the light? It keeps shining. The mind's just a flicker, a projection, not the real deal.

Key Realization: The Mind as a Shadow of Consciousness

So, the mind's not some solid chunk of you—it's a ripple, a shadow cast by consciousness. When the body checks out, the mind waves goodbye too. But consciousness? It's not going anywhere—it's the one thing that doesn't pack up and leave.

The True Nature of Memories: Imprints, Not You

The fear of losing all memories forever is rooted in the false identification with the mind and body. In reality, memories are like waves on the ocean of consciousness—arising, shifting, and eventually subsiding. They are temporary patterns within awareness but do not define it.

What we truly love about others is not their memories but the consciousness that animates them. This means that the essence of what we love can never be lost because consciousness is timeless and unchanging.

It's like getting attached to the shape of different windows rather than admiring the light shining through them.

The Continuity of True Memory: Beyond the Mind

Non-duality says it's not the memories of loved ones we lose—it's their essence, that alive-ness, that matters. We panic thinking they're just body and mind, gone forever. But if consciousness is one big, eternal thing, then what we love—their spark—doesn't vanish. It's still here, just not boxed in a person anymore.

Final Thought: Who Is Aware of the Mind?

Instead of asking, "Where is the mind? "Ask: "Who is aware of the mind?"

You will say: "I AM."

When a thought arises, who notices it?

When a memory appears, who sees it?

When emotions fluctuate, who is aware of the fluctuation?

The answer is simple: It's you—not the 'you' with a name and a driver's license but the quiet, endless awareness that's always been.

This awareness doesn't come and go. It's the one constant, the one light that reveals every thought, memory, and emotion without being touched by any of them.

In the end, it's not about tracking down the mind—it's about seeing that you're the ocean, and the mind's just a wave doing its thing.

BY DAVID ENGLAND

1. Why Can People Still Experience Without a Functioning Brain?

The brain's like a phone screen—smash it, and the signal's still there. Consciousness isn't made by the brain; it just flows through it. When the screen's off, the real juice—awareness—keeps humming.

2. Why Do Some People See Heaven or Hell in NDEs?

People experience different visions based on their mental conditioning, beliefs, and expectations. It's like dreaming—you can only dream within the limits of what your mind has been exposed to. It's your mind's mixtape playing its hits. If you've got 'heaven' on repeat, that's the vibe you get. Scared of hell? That's what shows up. Near-death stuff's a dream remix, not the final track.

NDEs aren't glimpses of final realities but temporary projections of the mind's deep-seated beliefs.

3. Does This Mean Hell Could Be Eternal After Death?

This is where non-duality flips the script. No experience is permanent—whether good or bad. If hell were truly eternal, no one could ever return to speak of it. A nightmare feels real while you're in it, but eventually, you wake up.

4. What Happens at the Final Death?

When the physical body dies, the gross body dissolves, but the subtle body might carry forward impressions for a while. Eventually, all impressions are transcended, leading back to Pure Consciousness (Atman).

A wave might rise and fall, but it's never separate from the ocean. When it dissolves, it's just water—never really separate in the first place.

Death is not an eternal heaven or hell but a return to the infinite, non-dual awareness.

Final Answer: How Can Someone Experience Without a Brain?

- **The subtle body remains active,** even when the physical body shuts down.
- **NDEs are temporary mental states,** not final destinations.
- **Consciousness remains the constant,** beyond body and mind.

In the end, it's not about what the mind projects—heaven, hell, or anything in between—but about realizing that you are the awareness that makes all experiences possible.

WAKING, DREAMING, SLEEPING... WATCHING

You live three lives every day. One where you're awake. One where you're dreaming. And one where everything seems to disappear.

Vedanta calls these **Jagrat** (waking), **Svapna** (dreaming), and **Sushupti** (deep sleep). Three different worlds, each one feeling real while you're in it. But what do they say about *you*?

Let's take a closer look.

The waking state, or Jagrat, is the one you're most familiar with. The "real world." You get up, check your phone, brush your teeth, pay bills, get annoyed in traffic, and maybe laugh with a friend or two. This is the state where your senses are fully online. You see, hear, touch, taste, smell. But here's the trick: you don't question it. You call it "reality" just because your eyes are open. But was last night's dream any less real when you were *in* it?

When the senses shut down, the mind kicks into high gear. It spins stories out of memories, hopes, and fears. You become the actor, director, and audience all at once. You run from things. You fall in love. You fly. You cry. Then you wake up and say, "Oh, that was just a dream." But if it felt real *then*, and you only realized it was a dream *after*—what does that say about this waking state? What if it's just a longer dream?

And then there's deep sleep—Sushupti. This is the mystery state. No thoughts. No dreams. No world. No "you" to remember anything. It's total stillness.

And yet…You say, "I slept well." How do you *know* you slept well if "you" were gone?

Because something was still there. Still watching. Still present.

That's what Vedanta calls **Turiya**—the Fourth. Not a fourth state, but the ever-present background behind the other three.

Waking and dreaming are full of content—stories, sensations, experiences. Deep sleep is contentless—but not unconsciousness. **Consciousness never shuts off.** It's the screen behind all three movies. You, the real you, are that screen. Not the actor on it.

The dream ends. The world changes. The thoughts come and go. But you—the silent witness—don't.

Here's a thought experiment:

If you're the same person who woke up this morning…

And the same one who had a dream last night…

And the same one who "slept like a rock" last weekend…

Then *who* was there through all three?

Who's the one constant?

That's the question that breaks the illusion.

You've never actually been "unconscious." You've just moved through different modes of experience. But behind each one is the same presence—still, silent, untouched.

You've never not been you.

Even when the mind shut off.

Even when you forgot your name.

Even when the body was still.

That presence?

That's what you are.

Not the waking person.

Not the dream character.

Not the sleeper.

But the one watching it all unfold.

BEFORE BIRTH, BEYOND DEATH

People often ask, "What's the meaning of life?" Yet rarely do they ask how they even know what life is. How can one seek to understand the meaning of something they don't fully comprehend—something they're still in the middle of experiencing?

Even more puzzling, we speak with confidence about death—an experience we haven't had. Or... have we?

Let's take a step back.

Before you were born, do you remember anything?

Most would say, "Of course not. I didn't exist yet." But that assumption reveals something deeper—it assumes that experience is tied to memory, and that consciousness must begin at the moment you can recall it. But does it?

You were alive in your mother's womb. Your heart beat. Your body formed. And when you were born, people celebrated your arrival. You existed. Yet most can't remember anything before the age of two or three.

Does that mean you were dead during those years? Of course not. You were simply alive… without self-awareness.

So why do we assume that the absence of memory after death means a total absence of being?

This brings us to a deeper question: When did your existence actually begin?

Was it the moment of birth? Conception? In your father's seed? Your mother's egg? Your grandparents'? Your great-grandparents'? If you keep tracing the lineage, you start to see: there is no clean beginning. You are the continuation of something far older than your name, your face, or your body.

And what about death? We fear it because we associate it with the end of experience. But ask yourself: Did you fear anything before you were born?

You didn't. Because fear only arises in the waking state—when there's a "you" with an identity to protect.

In sleep, your fears vanish. In deep sleep, you don't mourn the loss of your body, your loved ones, or your plans. You dissolve into a state of pure being—no identity, no worry, no story. And yet, you still wake up. Something was there, even in the nothingness.

What is that?

People claim they will experience heaven or hell after death. But who or what will experience it? If you say "you" or "I," then ask: Who are you exactly?

BY DAVID ENGLAND

Are you the body? The name? The thoughts? All of those are temporary—and all of them change. So what remains?

Let's go deeper.

You only see because you have eyes. You hear because you have eardrums. You touch because of nerve endings. You smell because of a nose. You taste because of a tongue. Your entire experience of the world is filtered through the five senses—and all of them rely on one fragile machine: the body.

But the body dies.

So if the body ceases and with it your brain and senses, what mechanism remains to experience anything at all?

Some argue that we have "spiritual senses" or a "glorified body" awaiting us. But that leads to more questions: Where was this eternal body before you were born? Why would your soul suddenly become immortal after being born into a fragile, limited body that forgets its origin?

Wouldn't that suggest your immortality had a beginning? And anything that begins can't truly be infinite.

Now pause and consider this:

When you dream, wild things happen. Entire worlds unfold. You see, hear, run, fly. But your body is asleep in bed. So who experienced the dream?

Close your eyes. Imagine an apple. Who saw that image, when your eyes were closed?

Think a thought without saying a word. Who spoke it? Who heard it?

These questions point to something deeper than the body—the Witness. The one who sees, not with eyes. The one who knows, even without memory.

That Witness was there before you had a name.

And it will remain, even after the name is gone.

The body limits you. It's vulnerable. It's temporary. But you? You are not the body.

From the moment we're born, we forget our true nature. We become entangled in stories, beliefs, and identities—most of which were given to us by others. We inherit religions, cultures, and worldviews like hand-me-down clothes.

And when the body dies, we panic. Because we've confused the outfit with the wearer.

But death is not the opposite of life. It is the opposite of birth. Life has no opposite. Because life is not what happens between birth and death—it is what makes both possible.

You don't fear non-existence. You fear the idea of it. And ideas only arise in the mind—while the mind is functioning.

Before birth, you didn't worry.

After death, maybe you won't either.

Maybe you'll just return to what you've always been.

BY DAVID ENGLAND

WHAT IS THE "EGO"?

The Character You Play in the Movie of Life

The word 'ego' gets thrown around in pop culture like it's just about arrogance or confidence. But what if I told you it's the very reason you suffer, judge, crave, and forget who you really are? This isn't about personality—it's about identity. It's that feeling of 'I' or 'me'—the part of you that says, 'Hey, I'm a separate person here.' It's like a little story your mind cooks up, a reflection of the real you—the pure consciousness, or the Self or Atman. Thing is, that story ends up clouding what's actually true about who you are.

(See Appendix C for a detailed explanation of the term Ego)

Life is like a movie, and the ego is the character you believe yourself to be. Your name, job, beliefs, memories, and personality—all these make up the role you play. Just like real-life actors can get consumed by their roles, we too become deeply identified with our character—forgetting who we really are.

Some actors become so immersed in their parts that'll they lose touch with their true selves. This is similar to how we get consumed by the worldly roles we play. But here's the thing: this isn't a flaw; in the apparent play of creation, forgetting is part of the game—so we may rediscover what never left.

The real you is the screen on which the movie plays—unchanging and untouched by the story. The ego isn't the enemy: it's just a role. The problem is we forget we're the screen and think we're only the character.

The word "persona" comes from Latin, meaning "mask"—the ego is like a mask you wear to interact with the world. Your true self is the face behind the mask—pure consciousness or awareness. Most suffering comes from forgetting you're wearing a mask and believing you are the mask.

The ego is also like a narrator that constantly tells a story about who you are, what you want, and what's happening. It's the voice in your head that says:

- "I need to succeed."
- "I'm not good enough."
- "They don't like me."

But here's the thing: the narrator is not you. It's just a voice-over. You are the one listening to the story, not the story itself.

Try this: Next time you hear that voice, pause and ask—who's listening to this? That question alone begins to untangle the illusion.

The Ego as a Shadow

Imagine a shadow on the wall. It looks real, but it has no substance—it's just a projection. The ego is like that shadow—it seems real, but it's just a projection of your mind based on memories, fears, and desires. This is why I used the "shadow" representing the Devil in the debate. The shadow has no independent reality; it's a projection cast by the light of consciousness.

Your true self is the light that creates the shadow—pure awareness. Most people cling to the shadows (the illusion) as if they fear the light, which is the very thing they are.

The Ego as Programs

The ego isn't a physical thing—no organ or object you can point to—it's like a set of programs or habits that run automatically in the mind:

- **Fear Program**: Avoid rejection.
- **Judgment Program**: Compare yourself to others.
- **Desire Program**: Seek pleasure or chase what's missing.

Most people live on autopilot, reacting from these programs without ever realizing it. But once you notice the program running, you've already stepped "outside" of it.

You're not the program; you're the one watching it run.

The Ego and Desire

Desire is the ego's fuel—it's what keeps the character running after the next scene. The ego craves pleasure, validation, or control, whispering, "If I get this, I'll be whole." But that's the trick: the ego can never be satisfied because it's built on the illusion of lack. Desire isn't wrong—it's just the ego doing its job, pulling you deeper into the movie. The catch is, you're already whole as the screen, not the character chasing shadows. When you see desire for what it is—a program, not your essence—you can let it play without being owned by it.

The Ego as Clouds and Costume

Your true self is like the sky—vast, still, untouched. Thoughts and emotions drift across it like clouds, but the sky never changes. Temporary thoughts and emotions pass by like clouds rooted in the ego. The problem arises when you identify with the cloud and forget you're the sky.

The ego is like a costume you wear on stage in the play of life. The true self is the actor who knows it's just a role. Suffering comes when you forget you're the actor and believe you're only the costume.

The Ego's Role

The ego isn't bad—it's a map, not the territory. A tool for navigating form—but never the truth of who you are. It's not evil or something to destroy; it's useful for playing the game of life. The problem is when the tool becomes the master and you forget who's holding it. The ego can help you interact with the world, but it becomes a prison when you identify with it completely.

The Big Picture

In simple terms:

- **The Ego** = The character you play in life's movie.
- **True Self** = The screen or the awareness watching the movie.

•   The whole point is to get lost in the character for a while, to play the game so deeply that you forget it's a game. The real awakening is when you realize you're not the character—you're the one playing it.

In the next section, we'll take a closer look at The Trees of Eden—not as a historical event but as a profound symbol of the universal human journey from unconscious unity to self-awareness. Here, the Tree of Knowledge stands as the gateway to duality, while the Tree of Life whispers of our true, undying essence. This is not just the story of two individuals in the past but of a cycle that unfolds in every being—a passage from pure, non-conceptual awareness into the birth of ego, self-identity, and dualistic perception.

As we peel back the layers of this ancient story, we may come to see that the so-called 'fall of man' was not a tragedy, but a necessary step in this awakening—a shift that stirs in each of us, marking the beginning of a journey back to the oneness that was never truly lost.

I chose Christianity's Adam and Eve story because it stands as one of the most beautifully structured symbols of this universal shift in consciousness—a testament to its enduring power, even for those who hold it dear, to guide us toward a non-dual truth. And when seen from this lens, it reveals that what we perceive as a struggle between innocence and sin is but a illusion we've mistaken for truth.

THE TREES OF EDEN —
THE BIRTH OF DUALITY

Beyond the Garden: A Universal Echo

This isn't about rewriting Genesis or picking apart scripture for sport. It's about looking through a wider lens — one that sees Eden not as ancient history but as a symbol of something all of us live through. the experience of being, before we knew we were. Think of your earliest days — before you had a name, before the idea of "me" existed. There was no judgment, no fear, no separation. Just warmth, sensation, hunger, light. A pure flow of life. That is Eden. Not a place, but a state — of wholeness, of unity, of undivided awareness. And in the center of that state? Two trees. The Tree of Life and the Tree of the Knowledge of Good and Evil. Not plants, but symbols. One represents the truth of what you are. The other marks the moment that truth fractures into identity — the birth of opposites. The awakening of the separate self.

The Baby Mind Before the Bite

Now picture Eve in that garden — not as a sinner, but as something closer to a child. A pre-conceptual mind. A being that hasn't yet split the world into "this and that," "good and evil," "right and wrong."

Genesis 2:17 says: "But of the tree of the knowledge of good and evil, thou shalt not eat of it: for in the day that thou eatest thereof thou shalt surely die."

Later, Eve repeats this to the serpent in Genesis 3:2–3: "We may eat of the fruit of the trees of the garden: But of the fruit of the tree which is in the midst of the garden, God hath said, Ye shall not eat of it, neither shall ye touch it, lest ye die."

She knows the words. She can repeat the instruction. But does she grasp its meaning? Imagine a one-year-old child lying in a crib. A parent places a cookie within reach and says, "Don't touch that." The tone is serious. The rule is clear. But the child has no concept of rules. No idea of obedience or consequence. Just the smell of the cookie and the pull of desire. The child reaches. The parent returns: "No!" And now — confusion. Not guilt. Not rebellion. Just shock. Because the idea of "wrong" didn't exist until the reaction defined it. That's Eve. She reaches not with intent to disobey but through the innocent pull of curiosity. Of instinct. Of not-knowing. And only after the bite — her world changes.

If you don't yet know what death is, then you also don't truly know life. There's just being—not defined, not contrasted, not measured.

It's like telling a small child it will die if it touches something dangerous. The child will simply stare up at you with wide, innocent eyes…

but the words carry no weight. Why? Because the child doesn't even know it's alive yet. Not really.

Think about it: when our mothers carried us out of the hospital, did we know we were alive? We existed, yes—but we didn't know it.

So let me ask you—do you remember the first word you ever spoke? Your first step? Your first bite of food?

Of course not. Because there was no "you" to remember yet. No ego yet to claim the experience. Just awareness—silent, present, undefined.

That's what Eden was.

The Paradox of Sin Without Knowledge of Sin

Here's the paradox: If Eve doesn't know good from evil until after eating the fruit, how can her action be morally wrong?

Genesis 3:7 says: "And the eyes of them both were opened, and they knew that they were naked."

Shame follows. Fear. Hiding. The birth of judgment. But these come after. Before the bite, there's no self-consciousness. No moral framework. Just presence. And yet — she's punished. But disobedience requires intent. Intent requires judgment. Judgment requires contrast. And the knowledge of that contrast only arrives after eating the fruit. So what exactly is she being punished for? If she understood the rule, then the fruit gave her nothing. If she didn't, then the punishment is unjust. That's the flaw in the literal reading. The punishment comes before the ability to perceive wrongness — which makes it not a moral failure but a transition. It marks the moment awareness begins dividing the world into this and that.

The Tree as Threshold, Not Trap

Why put the tree there at all? Why place something untouchable within reach, then curse the one who reaches? If God is all-knowing, why would He place a trap in front of a mind that doesn't yet understand? Was it a setup? A flaw? Or something deeper? Some say it was a test of free will. But can you truly choose obedience if you don't yet know disobedience? Can you choose between right and wrong if you don't yet understand either? Choice without contrast isn't choice — it's reflex. From the non-dual perspective, the Tree of Knowledge isn't a trap — it's a threshold. The first moment where the One splits into two — not physically, but psychologically. Before the bite: a seamless "now." After the bite: self and other. Judgment and comparison. Good and evil. Birth and death. The tree wasn't placed to test. It symbolizes the beginning of duality—not the end of innocence but the start of perception.

The Serpent: Not Satan, But the Inner Whisper

Genesis 3:1 introduces the serpent: "Now the serpent was more cunning than any beast of the field which the Lord God had made."

It's often interpreted as Satan — the deceiver. But Genesis doesn't say that. It simply calls the serpent cunning. It tempts, yes — but not with evil. With knowledge.

"For God doth know that in the day ye eat thereof, then your eyes shall be opened, and ye shall be as gods, knowing good and evil." (Genesis 3:5) And that's exactly what happens.

The serpent is not the devil in red—it is the first ripple of separation, the whisper that precedes ego. It doesn't *form* the "I," but it points toward it. It's the suggestion of identity, not identity itself. The whisper that says, "Maybe you're more than just being. Maybe there's more to see, more to want, more to become." It's not evil. It's identity, waking up. The serpent is the first flicker of duality — the voice that says, "I am this... and not that." It's the origin of the "I" thought.

The serpent is not the ego itself—but its first ripple. The whisper is not yet the "I," but it sets the stage for it. The ego is not born in one instant—it gathers, like clouds before a storm. The bite is the moment it takes over the sky.

The Serpent in Paradise: A Perfect Puzzle

But pause here — another layer unfolds. If Eden is paradise, a flawless garden of unity, why is the serpent there at all?

Genesis 3:1 says: "Now the serpent was more cunning than any beast of the field which the Lord God had made."

Cunning — sharp, sly, a spark of disruption. If this is perfection, how does something "evil" (as tradition often paints it) slip into the scene? And why does God, who shaped every leaf and breath, let it coil around Eve with words that unravel everything? It's a paradox: a perfect Eden with an imperfect guest. Like an adult pressing a curious child toward a forbidden edge — "You won't die... ye shall be as gods" (Genesis 3:4–5).

But what if this isn't a flaw? What if the serpent's presence isn't evil breaking in, but the One stirring itself awake? In Advaita's light, perfection isn't a still pond — it's the Whole dreaming movement. The serpent doesn't invade Eden; it's born there, a flicker of the "I" rising from the silence. Not a mistake to fix, but a thread in the tapestry — the first note of contrast in a song that needs no composer's desire, only its own unfolding.

The Moment Everything Changes

Genesis 3:6 says: "She took of the fruit thereof, and did eat, and gave also unto her husband with her; and he did eat." The awakening is mutual —shared, and symbolic of all humanity.

Verse 3:7 follows: "And the eyes of them both were opened, and they knew that they were naked…"

They knew. They became aware of self, of contrast, of separation. That's the "fall." Not from God — but into form. Not into sin — but into self.

What Did They Really Lose?

God's warning was clear: "For in the day that thou eatest thereof thou shalt surely die." (Genesis 2:17)

But they didn't die that day — at least not physically. So what died? Oneness. The seamless unity with all things. The sense of being part of the Whole. That dies when "I" is born.

The "death" was not physical—it was the death of unity. The moment they became aware of self, duality began. This was not a betrayal—it was the beginning of contrast. Later in Genesis 3:22, God says: "Behold, the man is become as one of us, to know good and evil: and now… lest he put forth his hand, and take also of the tree of life, and eat, and live forever…"

This suggests something profound: Adam and Eve were never immortal to begin with. The "death" threatened wasn't the loss of immortality. It was the loss of unconscious eternity — of existing without fear of death. They were always mortal. But they didn't know it. Until the bite.

Consequence, Not Condemnation

The verses that follow are heavy:

"Unto the woman he said, I will greatly multiply thy sorrow... in sorrow thou shalt bring forth children..."

"Unto Adam he said... cursed is the ground for thy sake... in sorrow shalt thou eat of it..." (Genesis 3:16–17)

On the surface, it sounds like wrath. Judgment. Punishment. But read it again through the lens of duality. Pain. Suffering. Struggle. These are not punishments for sin. They are the natural effects of seeing through a divided mind. Once you know contrast, you feel lack. Once you feel lack, you chase desire. Once you chase desire, you suffer. This is not divine vengeance — it's the cost of awakening into illusion.

The Tree of Life — Still Standing

Genesis 3:24 says: "So he drove out the man; and he placed at the east of the garden of Eden cherubims... to keep the way of the tree of life."

The Tree of Life is never gone—only hidden. You can't return to it through effort, because the one trying to return is the very illusion that veils it. You don't reach it. You remember it. You dissolve into what you never truly left. The Tree of Life is pure being. Always here. But not visible to the one who seeks from a place of lack.

The Serpent in Everyday Life:

What stirs when temptation calls — good, bad, or in-between? It's the same whisper behind every want: the illusion that something is missing.

Call it "sin" — cheating, greed, lies — and you might blame "the devil." It's easier to point outward than to face the pull within. But what about the rest? Craving a burger on a diet? Pushing for a dawn workout? Chasing a six-figure job? No Satan there, no God — just hunger, grit, ambition.

Here's the key: it's the same voice.

The serpent isn't a villain outside you — it's the whisper that precedes identity. The Ego is not born in the whisper but in the moment that whisper is believed. The moment awareness says, "I am this... and not that." "Ye shall be as gods, knowing good and evil" (3:5). Not evil, but the nudge of "more." It tempts to indulgence: "One bite won't hurt." To ruin: "No one will know." To triumph: "This job's your ticket." One root, many masks — always tugging you from now.

Take ambition: a dream gig beckons. "Risk it, you deserve more." Success, not sin — yet it's the same whisper. The ego lures to failure and to victory, judged "devil" or "drive" by the mind alone. It's Maya, the illusion of lack. "Eat the fruit — you'll be like God." "Get the job — you'll be enough." Same trick: you're whole, but it convinces you you're not. Genesis 3:7 seals it: "Their eyes were opened" — not to truth, but to "me" chasing "more."

The serpent didn't create deception—it reflected the mind's first ripple of desire. "Ye shall not surely die" (3:4) bends God's word (2:17) into desire's lens, trading unity for contrast. Without it, no choice, no pain, no growth — just being. It's not your enemy; it's awareness wearing a self. The dream of choice — real to the ego, unreal to the One — lets experience unfold.

The serpent is the suggestion of 'I'—not the ego itself, but the pull toward becoming someone.

Eden Was Never Behind You

This isn't the story of a woman long ago. It's the story of you. We all begin in Eden — pure presence. Then we taste the fruit — the world of identity, labels, and judgment. We leave the garden — not by force, but by forgetting. And we wander. But Eden isn't lost. The Tree of Life was never uprooted. It stands still, within you — behind the veil of thought, beyond the illusion of "I." Not something to reach. But something to see again.

You never left Eden. You only fell asleep in it. And now, you are waking up.

THE ILLUSION OF SEPARATION

Have you ever looked in a mirror and forget that the reflection isn't actually you? It's so convincing that you fix your hair, adjust your clothes, maybe even talk to it sometimes. But that reflection is just light bouncing off glass—it's not you.

Here's the twist: When you walk away, the mirror reflection disappears, but you remain. In the same way, what we call "separateness" is like the mirror's reflection—convincing but not real. The real you is the consciousness that sees the reflection, not the reflection itself.

We're so used to identifying with the reflection—the body, the personality, the labels—that we miss the one doing the seeing. The illusion of separation is powerful, not because it's real, but because we're so used to looking at the mirror that we never stop to question it.

In Vedanta, this illusion of being separate is called Māyā—it's like a veil pulled over our eyes by Avidyā (ignorance), making us mistake the temporary for the eternal, the many for the One.

To really get this, let's start with a simple analogy.

The Paper and the Hand: An Analogy for Separation

Imagine a piece of paper with a few holes punched through it and a hand with its fingers sticking through those holes. From above the paper, it looks like each finger is separate, independent, doing its own thing. But if you look underneath, you'd see that all the fingers are connected to the same hand.

Analogy 1:

The paper is Māyā—the illusion of separation.

The fingers are like individual selves—separate on the surface but really just expressions of the same reality.

The hand is consciousness (Atman)—the one true self that shows up as many.

The mistake we make is believing that the paper—the illusion—is what's real. We get so caught up identifying with the fingers that we miss the hand holding it all together.

In the same way, we go through life believing we're separate beings, cut off from each other and from God. But if we could see past the paper—if we could see through Māyā—we'd realize that all selves are just expressions of the same consciousness. We're not the fingers; we're the hand.

The Ocean and the Waves: Different Forms, Same Essence

Another way to look at it is through the analogy of waves on the ocean. Each wave seems separate, rising and falling with its own form and motion. But is it really separate from the ocean, or is it just the ocean showing up in different forms for a while?

Analogy 2:

The ocean is consciousness—limitless, formless, and always present.

The waves are like individual selves—temporary forms that appear separate but are never actually apart from the ocean.

When a wave merges back into the ocean, its shape vanishes—but the ocean itself remains unchanged. In the same way, when an individual life ends, only the personal form disappears; awareness itself persists.

The Mirror and the Reflections: One Light, Many Images

Imagine a room full of mirrors, each reflecting the same light source in different ways. Some reflections look bright, some dim, some are even distorted. The reflections seem separate, but the light making them visible is one and the same.

Analogy 3:

The mirrors are like individual minds, each reflecting consciousness in its own way.

The reflections are the experiences and identities that seem separate.

The light is consciousness (Atman)—the one reality behind all appearances.

The mistake we make is getting caught up in the reflections instead of recognizing the light. The reflections come and go, but the light stays constant.

In the same way, our experiences, bodies, and identities are temporary. But the consciousness that witnesses them—that's the real you, and it doesn't change.

The Dreamer and the Dream: All Within One Mind

Think about a dream where you're walking through a city, meeting people, feeling emotions. The city seems real, the people feel separate, and the emotions seem genuine. But when you wake up, you realize that the whole dream—the city, the people, even the version of "you" that was walking around—only existed in your mind.

Analogy 4:

The dream is Māyā—the illusion of separation.

The dream characters are individual selves—seeming separate but actually part of the same mind.

The dreamer is consciousness—the one reality behind all appearances.

The dream felt real until you woke up. In the same way, what we call "waking life" is just a dream projected by Māyā. When you wake up to your true nature, you realize the separation was never real—only an illusion created by the mind.

The Snake and the Rope: Mistaking the Form for Reality

There's an old Vedantic story about a guy who sees a snake in the dark and freaks out only to find out it was just a rope the whole time. His fear was real, but the snake wasn't—it was a projection of his mind based on ignorance.

Analogy 5:

The rope is consciousness—the one reality that never changes.

The snake is the illusion of separation—a projection of the mind.

The light that reveals the truth is self-knowledge—the realization that dissolves the illusion.

In the same way, the suffering we go through because of the illusion of separation feels real, but the separation itself isn't. It's just a misunderstanding—like mistaking a rope for a snake.

Seeing Through the Illusion: The Key to Freedom

All these analogies point to one simple truth: the separation we believe in is an illusion—just like mistaking the snake for the rope.

We're so used to identifying with the finger, the wave, the reflection, or the dream character that we miss the bigger picture—that all of them are just different ways consciousness shows up.

The real awakening isn't about becoming something different—it's about seeing through the illusion of separation and realizing what you've always been: the hand beneath the paper, the ocean beneath the waves, the light behind the reflections.

What we truly are isn't a separate self but the one consciousness that shows up as all things. The illusion of separation isn't something we need to destroy—only something we need to see through.

In the end, breaking the illusion of separation isn't about rejecting the world or other people—it's about recognizing that they're not separate from you in the first place. Once you see through the paper, the fingers stop appearing separate, and you realize it's all just the hand.

When the veil of Māyā is lifted, you see that what you've been searching for has been right here all along—hidden in plain sight, beneath the illusion of separation.

Many scriptures subtly point to the same truth Advaita Vedanta declares boldly: you cannot truly see God as something separate—because God is not an object. God is the very subject, the light behind the seer. When the Bible says "no one can see God and live," it's not about physical death—it's about the death of the separate self. Below are verses that reveal this truth, reinterpreted from a non-dual perspective that even Jesus hinted at.

Exodus 33:20

KJV:
"And he said, Thou canst not see my face: for there shall no man see me, and live."

Insight:
You can't see God and remain who you think you are. The ego must dissolve. True sight requires the seer to disappear.

1 Timothy 6:16

KJV:

"Who only hath immortality, dwelling in the light which no man can approach unto; whom no man hath seen, nor can see..."

Insight:

God is not something you walk up to. He's the light too close to touch—because you are that light. There is no "you" outside it to approach.

John 1:18

KJV:

"No man hath seen God at any time..."

Insight:

The separate mind cannot behold God—only the awakened Self knows the Source, not as a vision, but as Being.

1 John 4:12

KJV:

"No man hath seen God at any time. If we love one another, God dwelleth in us..."

Insight:

Love is God recognizing Itself in form. No one sees God—but when love flows, separation disappears.

Isaiah 6:5

KJV:
"Woe is me! for I am undone… for mine eyes have seen the King…"

Insight:
To behold God is to be undone. It's not visual—it's a collapse of who you thought you were.

Revelation 1:17

KJV:
"And when I saw him, I fell at his feet as dead…"

Insight:
This is ego death. The "I" falls away. Only silence and presence remain.

Matthew 5:8

KJV:
"Blessed are the pure in heart: for they shall see God."

Insight:
When the mind is quiet and the heart is clear, God doesn't appear as "other"—but as the light within all things.

Job 42:5–6

KJV:
"I have heard of thee by the hearing of the ear: but now mine eye seeth thee…"

Insight:

Realization makes all secondhand beliefs collapse. You don't just hear the truth—you become it. And the ego repents in dust and ashes.

This is what I love about self-inquiry—it's not about hearing about God—it's about realizing God directly, as your own Self.

Galatians 2:20

KJV:

"I am crucified with Christ: nevertheless I live; yet not I, but Christ liveth in me…"

Insight:

The false self is gone. What lives now is the One—the Self as Christ, the divine expressing through form.

These verses aren't denying God—they're denying the illusion of separation. To truly know God is to vanish as "me" and awaken as This. The "death" of the one who sees is not an end—it's the return to what has always been seeing.

THE PERSONAL AND IMPERSONAL GOD

Many people struggle with the idea of God being both personal and impersonal. Most religions describe God as having a will, emotions, and judgments, much like a human. But is this really the nature of the Infinite?

In Advaita Vedanta, God (Brahman) is not a person with preferences, moods, or desires. Instead, God is the fundamental reality—pure, unchanging, and beyond all attributes. The moment we try to define God in human terms, we reduce the infinite to something finite. People tend to personify God due to Genesis 1:27, which states, 'So God created mankind in his own image, in the image of God he created them; male and female he created them.' But what does 'in his own image' truly mean? Could it be referring to God's imagination, a reflection of divine consciousness rather than physical form? After all, why would an infinite, formless God require a body?

People also personify God because they lack the knowledge to conceive of divinity beyond human terms. They attribute emotions to God—anger, jealousy, love, and forgiveness—because that is the only way they know how to relate to the divine. But if God is the eternal, unchanging reality, then where would these emotions arise?

- If God is perfect and complete, what need would there be for emotions, which are reactions to change and circumstance?
- Can an unchanging being experience a change of heart or mind?
- If God feels anger or jealousy, what could possibly provoke such feelings in an all-knowing, all-powerful being?
- If God experiences love, is it not the same love that animates all of creation, flowing through every being, rather than an emotion held by a separate entity?

Perhaps the truth is this: God does not 'feel' as humans do but instead experiences through us. When we love, God is loving through us. When we grieve, God is grieving through us. When we awaken to joy, it is God awakening to joy within creation. The divine essence permeates all, not as a personal deity reacting to the world but as the ever-present consciousness witnessing itself through every experience.

If one believes God has desires, then who are you praying to? Why would you pray to a God to fulfill your desires if that same God harbors unfulfilled desires of its own? If such a God existed, surely the desires of mere mortals would be insignificant to God. How could something finite offer anything to the infinite, when the finite itself exists within the boundless nature of the infinite?

What, then, is prayer? That... I'll leave for you to discover.

- God isn't jealous—jealousy arises within the mind.
- God doesn't fear anything—fear is a construct of the ego.

BY DAVID ENGLAND

- God doesn't cast judgments—judgment is born of dualistic perception.
- God doesn't have mood swings—fluctuations of emotion are movements within the mind, not of the Self.

But here's the profound truth: God (Brahman) experiences it all through you.

Brahman (the absolute reality) does not need to experience, for it is beyond experience and expression. However, through creation, the play of duality unfolds, allowing consciousness to manifest in countless forms. This does not imply a need or desire in Brahman but rather a spontaneous expression of its infinite nature.

The eternal encompasses all space—it is boundless, without beginning or end. Sit with that. Think about it deeply until it makes you feel weird—until the mind stretches to grasp what cannot fully be grasped. Because in that discomfort, in that unease, you may catch a glimpse of the truth beyond perception: that God is not an entity to be appeased but the essence of experience itself.

In this understanding, Creation isn't something God experiences from the outside—it is the infinite experiencing itself from within. It is like a mirror reflecting infinite possibilities, yet the mirror itself remains unchanged. What we call experience is simply the reflection of consciousness within the field of duality.

Think about it:

- Electricity powers everything from lamps to computers, yet it has no personal agenda. It doesn't choose who gets light or power—it simply flows whenever the circuit is complete.

And if misused, you get a zap, whether it's a curious toddler or a criminal.

- Gravity doesn't care who you are. If both a saint and a sinner jump off a building, they'll fall at the same rate. Gravity makes no moral distinctions—it simply obeys its natural law.
- The sun shines on all without discrimination. It doesn't decide who is worthy of light—it just radiates. *"He causes his sun to rise on the evil and the good, and sends rain on the righteous and the unrighteous."* —Matthew 5:45

Likewise, God is not an external being who picks and chooses who to bless or punish. God is the very essence of existence itself. The "personal" aspect of God—love, compassion, creativity—actually manifests through each of us. Any human traits we project onto the Divine are ultimately reflections of our own nature.

The Duality of Experience: Why Everything Must Exist in Contrast

Every situation, event, action, and circumstance in this world exists within duality—that is the entire structure of experience.

- **What did you experience before this life?** Exactly. You have no recollection, no contrast, no form. Then the ego is born—and with it, the experience of contrast: light and dark, joy and pain, love and fear—because duality is the very mechanism through which life is known.
- **Would you recognize peace if you had never known struggle?** Would pleasure mean anything without pain?

Duality is not a mistake—it is the way experience unfolds. But once we recognize it for what it is, we can see beyond it to the deeper truth: that all opposites arise from the same source.

The Mind's Escape Hatch:
"Some Things We're Not Meant to Understand"

When presented with questions that challenge how they believe or questions they cannot answer without contradiction, many people resort to phrases like:

- *"Some things are beyond human understanding."*
- *"God works in mysterious ways."*
- *"We're not meant to know everything."*

I used to do this a lot myself! When I was caught in the grip of the Shadow, I didn't even realize I was avoiding the very questions that could set me free. But once I started paying attention, I noticed something strange—almost everyone was saying the same thing. It was as if we all had the same program installed, called:

"Thinking for Yourself?" – (That Function Has Been Disabled)

"Do Not Question—God Will Punish You" – (Warning: System Lockdown Imminent)

It's as if the moment someone starts to ask real questions, a mental firewall kicks in—shutting them down before they can even consider an alternative perspective. But here's the thing: If the truth is so fragile that it can't be questioned, was it ever really truth?

Would you tell a child not to explore, not to think, not to question the world around them? Of course not. Because discovery leads to growth. Yet, when it comes to the biggest questions of existence, people have been trained to avoid them—like a self-imposed thought prison.

But let's flip the script for a second:

- If God is infinite, then why would questioning reality be dangerous?
- If truth is truth, then why would seeking it be punishable?
- If understanding was never meant for us, then why were we given the ability to think so deeply?

These questions aren't blasphemy—they are the very reason you are here. The mind is not a prison, unless you make it one.

No great discovery, no deeper realization, has ever come from choosing not to understand. Every great leap in knowledge—whether spiritual or scientific—came from questioning what others blindly accepted.

- Imagine if the first humans had said, *"Fire is mysterious—we're not meant to understand it."*
- Or if scientists had said, *"We'll never understand space—it's beyond human reach."*

Choosing not to understand is not wisdom—it is avoidance. The truth is, we can understand far more than we've been led to believe. The problem is not the impossibility of knowing—it is that most people never challenge what they've been conditioned to accept.

Instead of saying, "No, you're wrong," consider this an invitation: Question deeply. Follow every contradiction to its root. Does it logically hold up? Or does it collapse under its own weight?

The Trap of Personifying God

People naturally try to relate to God as if God were a being like them. This is why God is often described as having emotions—love, anger, jealousy, patience. This tendency to project human emotions onto God is called anthropomorphism.

This is why in some religious traditions, people say things like:

- *"God is testing you."* As if God is a teacher handing out exams.
- *"God is angry at sin."* As if God experiences emotions like humans.
- *"God has a plan for you."* As if God is a person micromanaging individual lives.

But does an infinite, all-encompassing reality need emotions, plans, or judgments?

No. These are human concepts. The idea of an angry, punishing God is just a projection of human fear and misunderstanding.

The truth is, God is beyond all attributes. The moment you assign a personality to God, you are no longer talking about the Infinite—you are talking about a limited concept that exists within your mind.

Just as the ocean does not have a preference for which waves rise and fall, God does not "decide" who succeeds or fails. God is simply being, and it is within this being that everything—including our free will—arises.

Beyond the Personal and Impersonal

So, is God personal or impersonal? The answer is both and neither.

- **Personal:** In the sense that love, intelligence, and creativity arise from this infinite consciousness and express through us.

- **Impersonal:** In the sense that God is not a separate being making decisions—it is the very fabric of existence itself.

When you stop trying to fit God into a human mold, you begin to see the truth: God is not a person watching over you. God is the awareness through which you are watching.

THE ILLUSION OF TIME: PAST, PRESENT, FUTURE

Time is one of humanity's greatest constructs. It serves as a practical tool, allowing us to measure, organize, and navigate our physical world. Clocks tick, calendars turn, and seasons change, giving structure to our lives. But beyond this practical level, time is nothing more than a mental construct—a framework through which the mind experiences reality. While the clock may divide existence into past, present, and future, consciousness itself is timeless. The present moment is the only reality. The past is a memory, a shadow of what was, and the future is nothing more than imagination, a projection of what might be. Yet, we often find ourselves trapped in these non-existent realms, weighed down by regret for what has passed and anxiety for what is yet to come.

Ask yourself this: Have you ever actually been to the past? Think carefully. You may recall a memory, but when that memory surfaced, where were you? **Still here—in the now.** The past can only arise as thought in the present. It is never experienced directly. So the next time your mind pulls you into a memory, remember: you didn't return to the past—you only brought a shadow of it into the now.

The now is all there is and all there ever will be. It is not in moving linearly between the past and the future. Past and future are mind-made. Time is a function of thought, not reality. Let this realization hit home, not just intellectually, but experientially. When you grasp this deeply, even for a moment, you begin to glimpse your timeless nature—the you that never moves, never ages, never leaves the now.

The Past and Future as Illusions

Imagine a river flowing steadily downstream. The water that has passed is gone, and the water yet to come has not arrived. The river is always in the present, always flowing. But the human mind, unlike the river, often clings to what has already flowed by and reaches anxiously for what is still upstream. This is the root of much of our suffering. Dwelling on the past traps us in guilt, regret, and nostalgia, pulling us away from the present reality. Likewise, when we project ourselves into the future, we fall prey to anxiety, fear, and the illusion of control. The mind creates endless what-if scenarios, many of which will never come to pass. We build entire stories around the unknown, missing the beauty and truth of what is right here, right now.

Time only appears real because we measure it in relation to change. But awareness itself does not change. The 'you' that observed your childhood is the same 'you' that observes now—yet your body, thoughts, and experiences have shifted completely. What, then, remains constant? That which is beyond time.

How Time Fuels Suffering

Suffering arises when we identify with the mind's stories about time. The mind uses the past to construct identity: "I am this because of what happened." It uses the future to build expectations: "I will be happy when…" Both are traps. In truth, you are not your past, and

BY DAVID ENGLAND

your future is not yet written. The only truth is now. Much of human suffering arises not from what is, but from thoughts about what was or what might be. Anxiety feeds on imagined futures; regret clings to remembered pasts. But as awareness grows, the weight of time begins to dissolve—and with it, the illusion that suffering must follow us wherever we go.

So how do we break free? It starts with stepping back into the now—a shift from being lost in the mind's stories to resting in the present moment.

Techniques to Ground Oneself in the Present Mindfulness

Bring your attention to the present moment. Notice your breath, your surroundings, and the sensations in your body. When thoughts drift to the past or future, gently guide them back to the now. Breath Awareness: Focus on the breath as an anchor to the present. The inhale and exhale are always happening now, providing a constant reminder of life's present flow. Feel the rise and fall of your chest, the coolness of the air as it enters, and let this rhythm draw you deeper into the stillness of this moment.

Presence Practices

Engage fully with whatever you are doing. Whether eating, walking, or listening, do so with full awareness. Allow yourself to be absorbed by the moment, letting go of the need to label or judge. Taste the food as if for the first time, hear the crunch of leaves underfoot, and let these simple acts become a doorway to the now.

Meditation Made Simple

Imagine standing on the side of a busy highway, with traffic passing in each direction. Now picture each vehicle as a thought. Don't try to identify the cars—don't pin down their make, model, color, or year—just let them pass without clinging to them. The same applies to thoughts during meditation. Simply observe them without attachment. If you find yourself "getting into a vehicle," meaning you latch onto a thought, it will take you down the highway—just as a thought can lead you down a rabbit hole of other thoughts. The trick is, don't try to force yourself not to think—because the moment you do, the mind runs wild. It's like someone saying, 'Try not to think of a purple elephant,' and boom, there's a purple elephant in your mind. Our minds are funny that way. So stay the observer, standing on the roadside of your mind, letting thoughts roll by like traffic without jumping in for the ride.

A Deeper Understanding

In Vedanta, time (Kala) is considered part of the illusion (Maya) that veils the truth of oneness. The eternal self (Atman) exists beyond time, untouched by the cycles of birth, death, and rebirth. Buddhism emphasizes the concept of impermanence (Anicca), teaching that clinging to the past or craving the future leads to Dukkha (suffering). The practice of mindfulness (Sati) is a direct path to freeing oneself from the tyranny of time. In Christian mysticism, the "eternal now" often takes center stage. Meister Eckhart, a Christian mystic, taught that the present is the only true moment—a timeless now that forever renews itself. This view points to God as ever-present, woven into each instant, where real connection to the divine unfolds only in the here and now.

A Practical Example: A river does not hold onto the water that has passed, nor does it reach for the water yet to come.

It simply flows. Likewise, when we release our attachment to the past and our grasping for the future, we too can flow naturally through life—peaceful, present, and free.

The Illusion of Time and True Freedom

When we see through the illusion of time, we awaken to a new way of living. The mind becomes a tool for navigating the world, not a master dictating our reality. We begin to experience life not as a series of past memories and future projections but as a vibrant, ever-present now. In this space, peace is not something to attain in the future. It is the natural state of being. Joy is not a memory from the past. It is the fragrance of the present moment. And love is not something to search for. It is the essence of who we are when time fades away, leaving only the eternal presence of now. By living in the present, we reclaim our true nature—the unshaken, timeless awareness that watches the river of life flow, neither clinging to what was nor reaching for what is to come, but simply being, simply flowing, simply free.

WHERE IS GOD WITHOUT SPACE?

"In the beginning God created the heaven and the earth."
— Genesis 1:1

"In the beginning was the Word, and the Word was with God,
and the Word was God."
—John 1:1

Line them up—and a deeper layer begins to emerge. Genesis says God created, while John says the Word was God, and the Word was there in the beginning, and through this Word, all things were made (**John 1:3**). So which is it—did God create the world, or did the Word? John seems to answer: **yes**—because the Word was God. And if that's true… then what was spoken into existence was not something separate from God—it was God made manifest, God as vibration, God as frequency, God as creation. But what exactly *is* the Word? In Greek, the term is **Logos**—and it doesn't simply mean a spoken word like we think today. It's deeper. Logos means *reason, intelligence, meaning, thought*—it is the inner logic behind all things. In ancient philosophy, Logos was seen as the divine mind, the ordering principle of the cosmos. So when John says the Word was God, he's not describing a sound—but a conscious vibration, a divine thought made manifest. Not speech like we know it, but pure awareness expressing itself. The Word is not an instrument used by God, but **God thinking itself into form**—creation as God's own reflection. In this light, creation didn't just happen through the Word—it is the Word, and therefore is God. Now re-read Genesis: "And God said…" becomes not a command spoken across space, but a thought within God, appearing as reality.

The Word isn't a tool God used—it's God expressed, and creation isn't something outside of God—it's God appearing as form. Now that changes everything. If the Word was God, and the Word created all things, then what space was God in when He spoke?

Picture a voice breaking the void, calling light and life into form—where's it ringing from, what's it moving through? It's a simple question, but it tugs at something massive—something foundational. Let's follow this thread to its very end: if God is real, eternal, and beyond comprehension, then God should withstand any question, so let's chase this one to the root—and see what still stands.

The traditional view says God is eternal, infinite, unchanging, and outside of space and time—even Augustine said: **"God is not in time; time is in God."** But then the story shifts: we're told God resides in heaven—a place with gates, a throne, and a direction (**Revelation 4:1–2**). He speaks to prophets, sends angels, feels anger, loves deeply, regrets decisions (**Genesis 6:6**)—He moves, He acts, and He is said to be separate from His creation. Here's the question: if God is outside space and time yet separate from creation, then what is that separation made of? Isn't that a form of space, doesn't a separation require distance, and doesn't distance require time? This isn't an attack—it's a quiet wonder, a respectful inquiry—because if we say God is outside but also separate, then we've introduced a framework that God supposedly transcends, and that framework collapses under the weight of its own claim.

To speak is to create sound—sound is vibration, and vibration requires a medium, something to move through, like air or water, which requires space. If there is no space, there can be no vibration, no movement, no voice—yet we read: **"And God said, 'Let there be light'"** (**Genesis 1:3**). That's an action—action unfolds, word, then light, cause, then effect, a sequence, and sequence is time. Space and time don't operate separately—one pulls the other in—so now consider: if God is separate, outside, and speaks, then He's already inside a setup that includes space and time. Some may say, **"Well, He's supernatural—beyond space and time,"** and that's fair, but even the act of **"crossing over"** from beyond into creation implies movement, and movement implies a moment—that's still space and time. Walk from your chair to the window—that's space; it takes seconds—that's time. You can't move through space without time tagging along—they are fused, Einstein called it spacetime, one fabric: you bend one, you bend the other. Now think of heaven: it has form, a throne, a direction, a place—if you can move within it, then space is present, and if space is present, even a spiritual kind, then time is ticking, whether it's noticed or not. Now back to the claim: God is outside creation, but **"outside"** is a spatial word—it implies separation, a gap, and any gap is space, and where space is, time is not far behind. So to say **"God is outside of space and time,"** then to say **"He is separate"** cancels itself out—the separation is space and time, and to act across that divide is to be in it.

To make this clearer, let's look at the diagram below. It shows Point A as Heaven, with the triangle symbolizing the Pearly Gates and the heart symbolizing God's throne, connected by a white line that implies space and time within Heaven itself. Point B represents

Creation—the dimensions of space and time as we know it, depicted as a cluster of stars. The black line between Point A and Point B represents the gap, which also implies space and time. Notice the distance within Heaven, from the gates to the throne—that implies space, and any movement between them, like angels approaching the throne, implies time. So space and time exist not just between Heaven and Creation but also within Heaven. God's own realm isn't free of spacetime if we are viewing this with a dualistic lens.

The triangle represents the pearly gates, and the heart symbolizes God's throne. The distance between them illustrates both space and time.

Heaven

Creation: The 'Dimensions' of Space and Time

Point: A

Point: B

The gap between Point A and Point B signifies the emergence of space and time.

C

Figure 1: Diagram illustrating the perceived gap between Heaven (Point A) and Creation (Point B), which implies space and time, and thus duality. The label "C" is often overlooked and questions the container of both points, revealing that God, as the canvas, encompasses all—dissolving the illusion of separation, as noted: "God is the container."

Now, let's explore the words that try to capture the infinite. They're not wrong—they're just human attempts to describe what cannot be divided, using divided language. In Hebrew (Old Testament), "Olam" is often translated as "eternity," but it more accurately means "a hidden time," "a long duration," or "age," while "El Elyon," meaning "Most High," is a term of elevation—but to be "higher" implies verticality, direction, and place. In Greek (New Testament), "Aionios," used in John 3:16 and many others, is translated as "eternal," but it also means "age-lasting," denoting time, not its absence. In Arabic (Qur'an), "Al-Awwal" (The First) and "Al-Akhir" (The Last) imply sequence—first, then last—while "Al-Batin" (The Hidden) raises the question: hidden within what? Again, spatial language. These aren't flaws—they're fingers pointing at something real—but every time we say "God is separate," we've created a distinction, and every distinction demands space for it to be seen. And if there's space, there's time, and if there's time, then God is no longer beyond it.

Let's walk through the core contradictions—not as accusations, but as open doors. God is unchanging, yet acts: "Now leave me alone so that my anger may burn..." (Exodus 32:10)—anger rises, then calms, a shift that implies time. God is eternal yet speaks new things: "Let there be light" (Genesis 1:3)—new speech, a new event, which is sequence, and thus time. God is infinite, yet separate—to be apart means there's a gap, and a gap needs space, but space isn't infinity: it's a measurement. God is beyond space, yet places exist—Heaven, Hell, thrones, directions, gates, which aren't metaphors in traditional theology but literal locations. God knows everything, yet tests us: "Now I know that you fear God" (Genesis 22:12)—why test, if all is already known? Every one of these turns on separation, and separation requires space, and space folds in time. This isn't a flaw in God—it's a flaw in our perception.

Let's double down on spacetime, because it's the key to unraveling this. Einstein's theory tells us space and time are one fabric—you can't have one without the other. That's polarity: here vs. there, now vs. then. Polarity can only exist within duality, a framework of opposites. Any separation—like the gap between Heaven and Creation, or even within Heaven—requires spacetime, and thus requires duality. But if God is truly outside spacetime, as the traditional view claims, He can't be part of a dualistic framework. Duality depends on spacetime to define its distinctions. Without spacetime, there's no separation, no polarity, no opposites. What's left? Non-duality. If God is outside spacetime, the only answer is: God is non-dual. There's no other option.

Now let's picture this: God creates the universe—boom, everything we know: galaxies, atoms, space, time, energy, all spoken into existence. But where is it placed? If God is outside it, then the universe must reside in something—what contains it, where does creation sit? If it sits in a bigger "divine space," then that space is not God— it's beyond God, and if something is beyond God, He's no longer infinite. But if God truly is infinite, then there is no outside, no container, no gap, no place where God ends and something else begins.

So again, claiming that God is both "outside space and time" and "separate" from creation creates a contradiction. You can't be both infinite and separate, because to be separate, you have to be somewhere else. And "somewhere" is space—and space and time are fused together. This pulls God right back into the framework God is supposed to transcend.

Some might push back here, so let's address their arguments head-on and see what holds.

They might say: **"God is transcendent—He can act in space-time without being bound by it."** But acting in spacetime, like speaking **"Let there be light,"** implies sequence—word, then light. Sequence is time. And if God is **"outside"** but acting **"within,"** that movement across the gap implies a transition, which is spacetime. *Non-duality resolves this: there's no gap to cross, because Creation is within God, not separate.*

Or they might argue: **"Heaven is a spiritual realm, not a physical place, so it doesn't have spacetime."** Even a spiritual realm with structure—gates, a throne—implies distinction and movement. Moving from gates to throne is a spiritual **"space,"** and movement implies sequence, which is time. *Non-duality cuts through: there's no real structure, just appearances within the one reality.*

Another counter: **"God created spacetime itself, so He's not in it."** But the act of creation implies a before-and-after—no spacetime, then spacetime. That's a sequence, which is time. And what contains the created spacetime? If it's a larger space, God isn't infinite. If it's God, there's no separation. *Non-duality answers: spacetime isn't a separate creation; it's an appearance within God.*

They might claim: **"Separation is ontological, not spatial—God is distinct in being, not place."** But any distinction, even ontological, implies a **"not this"**—a limit. If God is infinite, there can't be a **"not God"** to be distinct from. *Non-duality says: the finite and infinite aren't separate; the finite is an appearance of the infinite.*

Finally, they might point to scripture: **"The Bible says God is separate—He's in Heaven, we're on Earth."** Scripture uses dualistic language to meet us where we are, but it points beyond itself. **John 1:1—"The Word was God"**—hints at no separation. **Isaiah 55:8—"My thoughts are not your thoughts"**—can mean God's infinite reality is what we're already part of. *Non-duality sees through the illusion of separation: what we call "Heaven" or "Earth" are mere appearances within the one infinite reality of God, not separate places.*

Here's another possibility—offered gently. What if God didn't stand apart from creation to make it? What if creation unfolded within God, not like a painter stepping back from a canvas, but like a painter whose brush, paint, canvas, and breath are all the same substance? What if there is no divide, no outside, no gap—only one reality, appearing as many? This isn't against faith; it's a deeper faith—one that no longer holds God at a distance.

This view also reframes the role of sin, which traditional theology uses to justify separation. Sin is seen as a divide—God is holy, we're fallen, so we're apart. But in non-duality, like in Advaita Vedanta, sin is ignorance—a misperception of our true nature. As I explored in "The Trees of Eden," the "fall" in Genesis isn't a cosmic divide but the birth of the ego, the illusion of separation. There's no real separation to begin with, so sin isn't a barrier: it's a mental veil. Realizing this unity dissolves the illusion of a gap between God and us.

Stand before a mirror. You see yourself—but reversed, distorted, not quite you, yet undeniably connected. Is the reflection separate from you? Yes... and no—it depends on where you're looking from. Creation may seem "other"—but it's just the reflection of the source. The mirror doesn't divide; it reveals. God isn't over there while we're down here—there is no distance, only one light reflecting as all things.

Ever had a dream so vivid that, while you were in it, you believed it was real? You walked down streets, saw faces, heard voices—every detail felt external, as if it existed "out there." Then you wake up and realize none of it was outside you: the cities, the people, even the spaces between them—all of it was in your awareness, a projection of your mind.

But notice something deeper: in that dream, you weren't just the character moving through scenes—you were the streets themselves, every person you met, and the one having the dream all at once. Your awareness split itself into many roles—the dream environment, every other character, and the main protagonist experiencing the dreamscape. In other words, your own mind—or pure awareness—was playing every part.

Now take that one step higher: God isn't a separate observer of creation—God is both the dreamer and the dream, expressing as every person, place, and thing. Just as your awareness becomes the entire dream when you sleep, the Infinite does the same in waking reality. Everything you see, feel, and experience is simply an aspect of that one boundless awareness playing as form.

People say, "God is beyond understanding," which often means: stop asking. But maybe the real mystery isn't something we need to protect from questions—maybe the real mystery is what's left when we remove every contradiction. God isn't confined to heaven, doesn't need a direction, doesn't need time, and doesn't exist in a gap between Itself and creation. God simply is—as all that is. There is no separation; there never was. And the more we try to locate God "somewhere else," the further we wander from the only place God ever truly is: here, now, everything.

This perspective isn't new—it echoes ancient wisdom. In Advaita Vedanta, all is Brahman, the one infinite reality, and separations are maya, illusion. Even in Christian mysticism, voices like Meister

Eckhart whisper the same truth: "The eye with which I see God is the same eye with which God sees me." There's no divide. God is the canvas, the container, the oneness behind all appearances. Spacetime, with its dualistic polarity, can't hold the infinite. Only non-duality can.

But this isn't just a logical conclusion—it's a lived truth. In my own journey, after 28 years as a Christian, the dualistic view never fully resonated. It was in exploring non-duality, through Advaita Vedanta, that I began to feel the unity I'd been seeking. In moments of stillness—whether through meditation or simply sitting with the world—I've sensed it: a quiet dissolution of "me" and "other," a glimpse of the infinite where there's no separation, just one seamless reality. It's not something I can prove, but something I know, like a memory of Eden before the bite. Advaita often emphasizes this direct experience—jnana, the knowing beyond thought. For me, non-duality isn't just the answer to spacetime's contradictions: it's the felt truth of what God, as the infinite, truly is.

A DEEPER LOOK INTO HEAVEN

Heaven's got a strong pull, doesn't it? The idea of a place where everything's perfect—no pain, no suffering, just bliss and God's presence forever. That vision runs deep in a lot of religious traditions. Streets of gold. Angel choirs. Eternal peace. But here's the thing—if God is truly infinite and eternal, then putting Heaven on a map—whether physical or metaphysical—starts to unravel.

From the lens of Advaita Vedanta, the whole framework of a "place" called Heaven is already caught in the illusion of duality. A separate realm? With boundaries? That alone makes it finite. What we call 'finite' is simply the Infinite wearing form—like a wave is still ocean, or a dream is still mind. The appearance of limitation doesn't mean there's a second thing—it just means the One is playing as many.

The Illusion of a Separate Heaven

Most religions imagine Heaven as a reward—some realm "out there" that you earn after death if you play your cards right. But separation itself is **Maya**—the illusion. Heaven as a destination reinforces the idea that God is in one place more than another. That right there sets up a contradiction: How can the all-pervasive be localized?

Advaita doesn't see Brahman—God—as a being who lives in Heaven. It sees Brahman as the *only* being. The ground of everything. So if Brahman is everything, where exactly would "Heaven" be?

The Problem with Eternal Time

People call Heaven "eternal." But usually what they really mean is: a very long time. A timeline that never ends. But real eternity isn't just endless time—it's **timelessness**. It's the **Now** beyond the ticking of clocks.

Think about it: to say "souls enter Heaven" implies movement, change, a before and after. But that's time. And time is part of Maya. So how can the eternal God—beyond time—create a Heaven that depends on time?

You can't step into eternity. You wake up to it.

The State Before You Were Born

Here's something most people don't consider: The state of Heaven is a lot like the state you were in before you were born—or more specifically, before the birth of your ego.

No name.

No labels.

No past to regret or future to chase.

There were no distinctions yet—and without distinctions, there was no suffering. Just undivided presence. No self-image to protect. No "me" and "God." No "this is mine" or "that's yours." That state wasn't empty. It was *whole*.

That's the essence of true Heaven—not something new to attain but something ancient we forgot.

Communion or Realization?

The dream of Heaven usually involves meeting God, face-to-face. That's beautiful—but still duality. *You* and *God*. Two. In Advaita, the highest realization isn't about meeting God—it's realizing **Tat Tvam Asi**—"Thou art That."

Heaven isn't when you finally reach God. It's when you realize you've *never* been separate. You were God, dreaming of being lost.

That's not a reunion. That's an awakening.

The Reward Trap

The traditional Heaven is built on a reward system—live right, believe right, and you get the prize. But that turns spirituality into a transaction. That's not love. That's bartering.

Real liberation (*Moksha*) isn't earned. It's *remembered*. It's not a carrot at the end of the stick—it's the stick being dropped altogether. There's no ledger. No waiting room. Just the dropping of illusion.

So What *Is* Heaven Then?

It's not clouds. It's not choirs. It's not even peace in the usual sense.

Heaven is Oneness.

Heaven is realizing there's nothing to chase, nothing to prove, nothing to fear. It's when the ego dissolves and the separate self stops pretending to run the show. You don't need wings—you just need to *see clearly*.

It's not up there. It's right here—beneath the noise, beneath the seeking, beneath the "me."

The moment you stop grasping for Heaven is the moment you see it's always been within you.

Going Beyond Heaven

Even the concept of Heaven—when taken literally—must be dropped eventually. Because it still divides. It still implies contrast. And anything that relies on contrast still belongs to duality.

The truth?

There's no Heaven to enter.

No Hell to escape.

No God to reach.

Only **Brahman**—appearing as all things.

Including you.

Including this.

BY DAVID ENGLAND

KARMA AND REINCARNATION

The Mechanics of the Self's Journey

1. Understanding Karma: The Law of Cause and Effect

Let's get one thing straight—karma isn't some cosmic punishment or reward system. It's not about a divine judge keeping score. Karma is just cause and effect, plain and simple. Every thought, action, and intention plants a seed that will sprout later—sometimes right away, sometimes way down the road. It's like gravity—it doesn't care if you believe in it; it just works.

- **Misconception:** Karma isn't fate. It's just the momentum of past choices rolling into the present.
- **The Law of Action and Reaction:** What you put out there comes back. Maybe not immediately, but nothing goes unaccounted for.

2. How Karma Fuels Reincarnation: The Three Bodies

Ever wonder why life feels like a continuous loop sometimes? That's karma doing its thing, keeping the cycle going until we wake up to what's really happening. This all plays out through the three bodies:

a. The Physical Body: Where Karma Unfolds

- **Temporary Ride:** Your body is just the vehicle through which past karma plays out.
- **Action Field:** This is where you take actions that create more karma, influencing what happens next.

b. The Subtle Body: The Baggage We Carry

- **What It Holds:** Your mind, intellect, memory, and ego.
- **The Luggage of Karma:** Your subtle body carries samskaras (impressions) and vasanas (tendencies) from past lives, shaping your desires, fears, and habits.
- **The Cycle Continues:** When your physical body dies, your subtle body takes these karmic patterns with it into a new life.

c. The Causal Body: The Root of the Problem

- **The Seed of Rebirth:** The causal body is where all unresolved karma and ignorance (*avidya*) are stored.
- **Why We Keep Coming Back:** As long as ignorance exists, the causal body ensures we reincarnate.
- **The Endgame (Moksha):** When self-knowledge dissolves ignorance, the causal body disappears, and so does the cycle of birth and death.

3. The Three Types of Karma: The Fuel for Rebirth

Understanding how karma works explains why we keep coming back:

- **Sanchita Karma:** The total karma from all past lives—like a massive storage unit of unfinished business.
- **Prarabdha Karma:** The portion of that karma you're dealing with right now in this life.
- **Agami Karma:** The new karma you're creating today that will shape future experiences.

4. The Mental Plane and the Manifestation of Karma

- **Cause in the Mind, Effect in the Physical:** Your reality starts in your mind. Every thought, belief, and intention sets the stage for what unfolds in your life.
- **The Gym Analogy:** Think about getting in shape. You can't just go to the gym, move some weights around, and expect results. It starts mentally before it becomes physical. If your mind is still trapped in an unhealthy mindset, your body will follow suit. You have to align your thoughts and beliefs with your goal—discipline, motivation, and mindset come first, then the results you imagined mentally will appear physically over time. Just like you can't expect overnight transformation in the gym, karmic effects also take time to show up in the physical world. You don't see the muscles growing immediately, but with consistency, they do. Karma works the same way—your inner conditioning eventually shapes your outer reality.
- **Karma Works the Same Way:** If your inner world is chaotic, your outer world will reflect that. Change happens from the inside out.

5. The Illusion of "My Karma"

- **It's Not Personal:** There's no cosmic bookkeeper punishing or rewarding "you." Karma is just the universe balancing itself.
- **The Ocean and Wave Analogy:** A wave may seem separate, but it's just the ocean in motion. Likewise, karma isn't "yours" or "mine"—it's just how consciousness moves.

6. Breaking Free: The End of Karma and Rebirth

- **No Doer, No Karma:** When you realize that you're not just the body or mind but pure consciousness, karma loses its grip. If there's no "doer," then who's accumulating karma?
- **Moksha (Liberation):** Once you wake up to this truth, the causal body dissolves, karma ends, and you're free. Like a wave merging back into the ocean, the illusion of separation disappears.

Reincarnation isn't an endless loop—it's a process fueled by ignorance. The moment you realize you were never separate to begin with, the illusion falls away, and you awaken to the timeless reality beyond karma and rebirth.

A DEEPER LOOK INTO HELL

Exposing the Myth of Eternal Damnation with Facts, History, & Logic

The Parental Fire Analogy:
Would You Do This to Your Own Child?

Many believers unknowingly perceive their love as greater than God's when they accept the doctrine of eternal hell. They believe that a so-called "all-loving" God will allow His creation to suffer in torment forever—but would any human with even the smallest amount of love do the same?

Let's put this belief to the test:

Imagine a couple with two children. One day, the father tells them both to do their chores before bed. One listens; the other does not. That night, a fire breaks out in the house. The father, awakened by the alarm, grabs his wife and rushes to escape. But instead of saving both children, he only saves the obedient one.

Outside, standing on the front lawn, the other child is trapped inside, screaming for help from a burning window. But the father turns his back and says:

"No. You disobeyed me."

He walks away as his own child screams in agony, consumed by flames—knowing full well he could have saved them but choosing not to.

"They had free will," the father says, his voice cold and detached. "I told them what to do. They made their choice."

If any human did this, we would call them a monster. So why do people accept this as divine justice from a God who is supposedly more loving than we are?

The overused argument—"Well, God gave you free will"—is weak and contradictory. Any sane, loving human would save both children regardless of their disobedience.

If a mere mortal parent can love unconditionally, then how could the definition of love (God) choose eternal abandonment over mercy?

Lets Dive Deeper...

How Many Times Does "Hell" Appear in the Bible?

Most believers assume that "hell" is all over the Bible, but in reality, the original scriptures never mention an eternal place of fiery punishment the way modern Christianity portrays it.

Let's break it down:

BY DAVID ENGLAND

The Old Testament (Hebrew Bible) contains zero mentions of hell as a place of eternal fire. Instead, it refers to Sheol—which generally means "the grave" or "the place of the dead." While Sheol is sometimes described as a shadowy realm where the dead exist (e.g., Isaiah 14:9-11), it is not a place of torment.

The New Testament uses three different words, but none of them mean "eternal fire where souls are tortured forever."

Word Used	Meaning	Times Mentioned	Origin
Sheol (שְׁאוֹל)	The grave; the realm of the dead. A place of silence and darkness where all the dead go, righteous or unrighteous.	65 times	Hebrew Old Testament
Hades (ᾅδης)	The underworld; a temporary abode of the dead. Often parallels Sheol in meaning.	10 times	Greek New Testament
Gehenna (γεένα)	A valley outside Jerusalem (Ge Hinnom) historically associated with child sacrifice and burning of refuse. Used symbolically by Jesus to warn of divine judgment.	12 times	Greek New Testament
Tartarus (τάρταρος)	Mentioned in 2 Peter 2:4 to describe a prison-like place for rebellious angels—not humans. Borrowed from Greek mythology.	1 time	Greek New Testament

*Note: The modern concept of "hell" as a place of eternal torment **does not directly match** any of the original biblical terms above. These words reflect **varied contexts**, including symbolic language, temporary holding places, and cultural metaphors—not literal eternal fire.*

What Did Jesus Actually Teach About Hell?

Most hellfire preachers quote Jesus to defend the idea of eternal punishment. But did Jesus actually teach about hell? Not in the way most think.

The main word Jesus used for "hell" was Gehenna, which was:

- A literal place—the Valley of Hinnom outside Jerusalem

- A garbage dump where bodies were burned
- A warning about earthly consequences, not afterlife punishment

Example:

"And if your eye causes you to sin, pluck it out. It is better for you to enter the kingdom of God with one eye than to have two eyes and be thrown into Gehenna, where 'the fire never goes out.'"

(Mark 9:47-48, referring to the ever-burning trash fires in Gehenna)

Jesus was using a real-world metaphor, not describing a supernatural torture chamber.

When Did Hell Become a Christian Doctrine?

The idea of hell as eternal torment wasn't originally part of Christianity—it was added centuries later as a tool for fear and control.

Historical Timeline of Hell's Evolution:

1. 1st Century (Jesus' Time) – No eternal hell. Jews believed in Sheol, a place of the dead, not torment. Jesus spoke of Gehenna, but as a metaphor.
2. 2nd-4th Century (Church Expansion) – The doctrine of hell begins evolving. Greek philosophical influences (like Plato's idea of an immortal soul) and Jewish apocalyptic literature shape Christian afterlife beliefs.
3. 5th Century (St. Augustine) – Hell becomes eternal punishment. Augustine, influenced by Roman law and the need to control converts, pushes the idea of hell as an eternal fate for sinners.

4. 13th Century (Dante's Inferno) – The fiery version of hell takes hold due to Dante's *Inferno*, a poetic vision of hell that people mistakenly take as theology.
5. 16th Century (Protestant Reformation) – Martin Luther and John Calvin reinforce hell as eternal punishment, keeping fear as a tool for obedience.

The modern concept of hell is NOT based on Jesus' teachings but on later church doctrine, Greek philosophy, and medieval literature.

The Contradiction of Eternal Hell & God's Love

Here's where the belief in eternal damnation collapses under its own contradiction:

- If God is all-loving, then eternal torture makes no sense. Love doesn't abandon its creation forever.
- If God is all-powerful, why not create a better system? A truly omnipotent being wouldn't need to rely on eternal suffering as "justice."
- If a human parent wouldn't do it, how could God? Any decent parent would rescue their child regardless of disobedience.
- If justice is eternal, why does sin have a time limit? If you sin for 70 years, why does the punishment last forever? That's not justice—it's divine cruelty. That's like receiving 3 life prison sentences for running a stop sign.
- If we are made in God's image, why is our morality superior to His? Humans forgive. Humans show mercy. If God is greater than us, why is His "love" weaker than ours?

Final Truth: Hell is a Human Creation, Not a Divine Reality

The fear-based doctrine of hell was manufactured by religious leaders, shaped by Greek philosophy, and popularized by medieval writings—but it is not scriptural truth.

The greatest fear-based deception of all time is the illusion that a loving God would cast His own creation into eternal suffering.

"There is no hell except the one we create within our own minds."

"We are not punished for our sins, but by them."

"Hell is not a place; it is the absence of awareness of oneness."

Most will continue to believe this because they fear that if they are wrong, they will burn for eternity. But ask yourself this: What exactly is going to burn? Your body? It will already be in the dirt, decaying—nothing more than bones and dust. Your soul? How can something that is non-physical, beyond matter, and inherently eternal be consumed by flames?

And if the soul endures, then what's the point of a resurrected body? If sensations, pain, and pleasure can be experienced without the physical senses, why drag the body back into the equation? Does God, the infinite and formless, really need flesh to deliver judgment? Would an all-knowing creator resort to barbaric, earthly tactics like fire and brimstone to prove a point?

The Self-Righteous Shadow in Disguise

Look around today and you'll see people holding signs that say, "Time is running out. Repent or burn in hell." They often mean well—but what they don't realize is that they are pushing people *away* from God, not toward Him. That sign doesn't say "God is love." It screams, "I'm righteous, and you're not."

Whether they realize it or not, they are acting out of fear, not love. Their message, though cloaked in morality, implies that God plays favorites—that He saves some and tortures others forever. But who decided they were fit to carry that message? If they truly believed God's love was unconditional, would they resort to threats and fear tactics? Their voice echoes not the Divine—but the very shadow they claim to warn against.

Years ago, I asked myself: *If someone were holding a sign for the devil, what would it say?* And the answer shook me. It wouldn't be crude or obviously evil. It would be nearly the same sign—because nothing keeps people further from God than fear posing as truth. This is fearmongering disguised as salvation.

The classic escape is: "Well, God gave us free will." But I covered this deeply in the debate titled *Free Will or God's Will.* Free will does not justify eternal torture. It is not love to offer someone fire and call it a choice.

Those who stand on street corners preaching damnation are often unaware that their shadow is louder than their message. It's not holiness—it's ego disguised as concern. They preach to feel right, not to help others awaken. In truth, the ones who shout the loudest often fear the most.

Let's cut through the illusion. The fire described in scripture isn't literal—how could it be? It isn't your skin that burns but your sense of self. The torment isn't physical: it's psychological, spiritual—the agony of clinging to the illusion of separation. The real "hell" is not a fiery pit but a state of consciousness—a prison constructed by your own mind, built brick by brick with fear, ignorance, and attachment.

Here's the truth: The flames aren't there to punish you: they're there to wake you up. They burn away what is false, what is temporary, what is not you. It is not your soul that burns—it is the ego, the identity, the story you've told yourself for so long. The flames are the heat of truth, and truth only hurts when you're attached to the lie.

Imagine this, You're not being thrown into hell. You're standing in it right now if you live in fear, if you live disconnected from God, from truth, from yourself. The eternal fire is not waiting for you on the other side—it is the present moment, consumed by a mind trapped in duality. And the only way out is not to be saved from the fire but to let it burn—burn away the false self until nothing remains but the pure, untainted light of awareness.

The real question is not whether hell exists but whether you are ready to walk through its flames—not to suffer, but to be set free.

The truth is, many are already living in hell, and they don't even realize it. It's not a place beneath the earth: it's a state of mind, a prison of perception.

Hell is when you wake up every day dreading what comes next. It's the anxiety that gnaws at your stomach before you've even stepped out of bed. It's the weight of guilt for things you've done—or things you failed to do—that clings to you like a shadow. It's the constant need for validation, the empty chase for fulfillment through material things, relationships, or fleeting pleasures.

Think about it: Have you ever achieved a goal you thought would make you happy, only to feel empty once you got it? That's hell. It's

BY DAVID ENGLAND

the endless cycle of craving and disappointment. You try to fill the void with distractions—social media, food, sex, work—anything to numb the quiet despair. But nothing works, because nothing external can fix what is an internal issue.

Hell is also living in the past, replaying every mistake and regret, or being lost in the future, paralyzed by fear of what might happen. It's being physically present but mentally absent, never truly living in the moment. It's when your mind becomes a battlefield, and you are both the prisoner and the warden.

Hell is not a physical place—it is a psychological state, a prison constructed by the mind. Many already live in this hell daily, not because they are punished by some external force, but because they are trapped in the illusion of separation. They exist in a self-imposed cycle of judgment, believing they are not enough—not worthy of love, success, or happiness. But this is not divine punishment; it is suffering born from illusion. The mind, caught in false beliefs, whispers lies about who they are, and because they accept these lies as truth, they remain bound to suffering. Hell is not something inflicted upon them—it is the unconscious repetition of their own conditioned perceptions.

Consider someone who is stuck in a loop of anger and resentment. They hold onto past betrayals, replaying old wounds over and over. Every time they see the person who wronged them, or even think of them, they are consumed by rage. But the person who hurt them has moved on—the only one still suffering is them. The chains of hatred bind only the one who holds them.

And what about those who constantly compare themselves to others? They scroll through social media, seeing only highlights of other people's lives. They feel inadequate, always behind, never enough.

They are in a self-imposed hell, burning with envy and self-loathing, trapped in a world of illusions.

This world will beat you down if you go through life not aware of this truth. Society is designed to keep you distracted, to keep you chasing things that do not matter, to keep you asleep. The world profits from your suffering, from your disconnection. Advertisers, media, even some religious institutions—they thrive when you believe you are broken and need something outside of yourself to be whole.

But the truth is, you are already whole. The hell you experience is not life's design: it is a product of the mind's conditioning. When you realize this, the flames lose their heat. The suffering dissolves. You step out of the illusion and into reality—not the harsh, painful reality that most see, but the true reality that lies beneath, filled with peace, understanding, and love.

Escaping this hell is not about dying and going to heaven. It's about waking up. It's about breaking free from the chains of your mind and seeing the world—and yourself—as they truly are. It's not the world that needs to change; it's your perception of it. When you shift your consciousness, the hell you once lived in becomes nothing more than a shadow—one that vanishes in the light of awareness.

LIVING ONENESS: COMPASSION AND MORALITY

Many people ask, "If there's no cosmic scorekeeper—no heaven, no hell—why shouldn't I just do whatever I want?" Let's explore that through the non-dual lens.

It's a fair and important question—especially if you're coming from a faith tradition like Christianity, or any system where right and wrong feel clearly defined, divinely issued, and deeply woven into your worldview. And it's not just Christianity.

Buddhism teaches the Five Precepts—guidelines like refraining from killing, lying, or stealing—not to appease a judging God, but to support inner clarity, compassion, and mindful living. Hinduism speaks of *dharma*—righteous conduct—and *karma*, the natural unfolding of actions and consequences. In both systems, morality flows not from divine threat or reward, but from alignment with truth, harmony, and the nature of reality itself.

So this isn't about rejecting morality—it's about reframing where it comes from and why it still matters, even when the idea of a cosmic scorekeeper is no longer part of the picture. Let's slow down—not to argue or dismantle your foundation—but to look at this question through a non-dual lens… and explore how morals still hold deep meaning when we realize everything is one.

In non-duality, There is no second thing. No real division between "good" and "evil," "light" and "dark," "me" and "you." It's all the same underlying essence, appearing in different forms.

That doesn't mean the world we live in becomes meaningless. It means the labels we use to divide it—good, evil, right, wrong—aren't ultimate. They're like calling water "hot" or "cold." The water itself doesn't change—only our experience of it does.

Same with life.

What one culture calls justice, another might call cruelty. What one moment sees as a blessing, another might later see as a curse. The non-dual view doesn't deny these differences—it just sees beyond them.

One may ask "But won't that lead to chaos?"

If you come from a dualistic tradition—where there's a cosmic judge, a moral ledger, a heaven and a hell—you might wonder: **"If there's no final judgment, then what stops people from doing whatever they want?"**

Here's the shift: **non-duality doesn't erase the human experience. It reframes it.**

Imagine life as a great play. On stage, there's conflict and beauty, joy and pain, virtue and betrayal. The characters take it seriously—but behind the curtain, it's all one production. Just because it's a play doesn't mean the characters don't care. In fact, **caring is what gives the story meaning.**

You're still in the story. You still feel, love, act, and choose. It all matters—but you no longer think it's the *whole* truth.

Why Morals Still Matter

So if good and evil aren't cosmic absolutes… why act ethically at all?

Because we're not floating in a void. We're here, with others. We're part of something.

Morality doesn't disappear in non-duality—it simply stops being transactional.

You don't love, forgive, or tell the truth because you're afraid of punishment or hoping for a reward. You do it because, when you realize we're not separate, care flows naturally like ripples in a pond spreading from the center of stillness.

Here's an everyday example:
Say someone cuts you off in traffic.

The ego flares—'How dare they!'

But awareness? It might wonder if they're racing to the hospital.

You still drive safely, maybe even more alert—but with compassion, not rage.

That's not moral law telling you how to feel. That's connection. That's awareness moving through you—not as a rule, but as a resonance.

When You See the World as Family

Think of it this way: When you find out someone is family—your brother, your grandmother, your child—you relate to them differently. You don't need a rule to love them. You love them because it feels true. That's the kind of care that arises when you see the world through oneness: not as strangers, but as shared being. And what you offer inwardly—your thoughts, your energy, your state—is what the world mirrors back to you.

Life doesn't react to you—it reflects you. Like a mirror, the world shows your inner state.

A mirror doesn't smile first. It only reflects the one you give it.

A Familiar Teaching, Seen More Deeply

Let's take a Christian angle for a moment. Jesus said: "Love your neighbor as yourself." He didn't say, "Do it or else." He pointed to a deeper truth: your neighbor is yourself at the level of spirit. Advaita would nod in full agreement. If we're all expressions of the same Self, then harming another is like harming your own hand. Kindness, then, isn't a rule—it's what flows when you remember what you are.

Do We Only Love Because of Fear or Reward?

Here's a reflective question—not an accusation, just something worth sitting with: If we need the promise of heaven or the fear of hell to "love our neighbor," is that really love? Is it love if it's tied to outcome? Or is it a kind of deal? This isn't to shame anyone—it's an invitation to go deeper. Because when we act from awareness rather than fear, our kindness becomes genuine, not just obedient. Our morality becomes resonant, not just imposed.

This is what I pointed to in the "Fish Love vs. True Love" chapter: If we love someone only for what they give us, is it really love? And if we act morally only because of reward or punishment, is it truly morality?

Letting Go of Absolutes Makes Morals More Real

This might sound strange at first, but here's how it lands for me: Letting go of moral absolutes doesn't make ethics meaningless. It makes them more meaningful. Because now, when you choose kindness, there's nothing to gain. No prize. No penalty. Only presence. Only connection. When there's no scoreboard, your goodness becomes pure.

I've felt this shift in my own life—not as some philosophy, but as a quiet change in how I move through the world. It feels lighter. Truer. Like breathing from a deeper place.

The Ego's Need to Divide vs. Awareness's Flow

The ego loves categories—right vs. wrong, good vs. bad, sinner vs. saint. It thrives on dividing. But from the view of awareness, those divisions soften. That doesn't mean we become numb to suffering or blind to harm. Quite the opposite. When awareness sees pain, it moves—not out of obligation, but out of love itself.

Like a mother rushing to soothe her crying child—not because she was "supposed to," but because she felt it in her bones. That's what moral action looks like when it flows from non-separation.

From Rules to Resonance

If you were raised on commandments and consequences, you might wonder: "What keeps me grounded without that structure?" The answer isn't lawlessness—it's inner alignment, a sense of balance, and the pull toward what feels naturally true.

The Ten Commandments say: Don't steal, don't lie. Advaita doesn't argue. It just explains why those things feel wrong: Because they disconnect you from your Self. When you lie, you build walls. When you steal, you fracture trust. These things feel off—not because they break rules, but because they break relationship. And when you see yourself in others, relationship is everything.

The Everyday Takeaway

Next time you feel triggered or tempted, pause. Ask: "Is this the ego talking—or shared awareness?" Let that question ground your next choice—remember, the ego wants to be right, but awareness seeks only what is real.

Morality, in non-duality, isn't gone. It's just no longer fear-based. It's how you flow with life when you know you're not separate from it.

THE PURPOSE OF SUFFERING

Suffering is one of those things that almost everyone questions at some point. Why do we suffer? If God is all-loving and all-powerful, why is there pain, loss, and conflict? For a lot of people, suffering feels like proof that something's wrong with the world—or that God's either not real or doesn't care.

But what if the real problem isn't suffering itself, but the way we understand it? What if suffering isn't a flaw in the design but a necessary part of it—like the shadows that make the light stand out?

What's ironic is that humans spend so much time asking "Why do we suffer?" while causing massive amounts of suffering to each other, to animals, and even to the earth itself.

- We hunt animals—not always out of need but sometimes for sport or tradition.
- We justify wars, revenge, and even cruelty when it suits us.
- We cut down forests, pollute oceans, and poison the soil—all while asking why life is so hard.

The real question might not be "Why does suffering exist?" but "Why do we think some suffering is justified and some isn't?" We're okay with suffering as long as it fits our story—when it doesn't, we call it evil or unfair.

The Cat and the Mouse: Who's Right?

Picture this: Let's say you have a pet cat and mouse. Picture your cat pouncing on your pet mouse. The mouse is scared, hurting, and soon, the cat eats it. Is the cat a villain? No, it's just being a cat, hunting like cats do. No malice, just instinct. But you would probably be upset at the cat.

Now imagine the mouse wasn't your pet and it was gnawing holes in your kitchen, eating your bread. You might cheer the cat on, toss it a treat, call it your little hero. Same chase, same ending, but to you, it's a win. So, what's true here? Is the cat good or bad? Depends on where you're standing. The cat, the mouse, you—it's all one tangled web, each part playing out its role.

Why the Mouse's Squeak Hits Home

You might shrug and say, "It's just a mouse—who cares?" Fair enough—we don't cry over every critter. But think about this: that mouse feels its fear as sharply as you feel a broken heart. Pain doesn't care who's feeling it—it lands hard, no matter the size of the body. A mouse's squeak and your quiet sob are different notes in the same song.

This isn't about saying a mouse's life equals yours in every way. Of course, you'd save your kid over a rodent any day. But at the root, suffering's suffering. It's all rippling through the same big pool of awareness—the one you're swimming in too.

Let's get real for a second. Imagine a world with no suffering at all—no pain, no bad weather, no conflict, no death. Sharks would swim up and nuzzle you like golden retrievers, lions would cuddle with gazelles, and nothing would ever get hurt. At first, it sounds amazing—a paradise. But if we look closer, that kind of world would come with some serious flaws.

1. Without Suffering, Nothing Has Meaning

If there were no pain, no loss, no struggle, then happiness, love, and peace would lose their meaning.

- Happiness without suffering is like light without darkness—you wouldn't even know you were happy because there would be nothing to compare it to.
- Love without the risk of loss would feel hollow. Loving someone gains its depth from the fact that you can lose them, that it matters.

It's the contrast that gives life meaning. Without suffering, everything would blend into one endless, flat line of neutral experiences—no highs, no lows, just a never-ending gray.

It would be like trying to paint a picture on a white piece of paper with a white marker—no matter how intricate or beautiful the design, it would be invisible.

The dark strokes aren't flaws in the painting—they're what make the image possible. In the same way, suffering isn't a flaw in life—it's the contrast that makes joy, love, and peace stand out.

2. No Death, No Evolution

A world without death sounds amazing—until you realize that death is what makes evolution, growth, and change possible.

- Without death, nothing would evolve. The same beings would exist forever, without adaptation, growth, or improvement.
- Ecosystems would collapse. If nothing died, the earth would quickly become overrun, resources would run out, and even plants wouldn't have space to grow.

Death isn't the enemy—it's the mechanism that makes life possible. Without it, existence would stagnate into an eternal, unchanging state—a kind of living death.

3. No Predators, No Balance

Imagine a world where lions, sharks, and wolves were all friendly. Sounds peaceful, right? But without predators, prey populations would explode, ecosystems would collapse, and diseases would spread unchecked.

- Predators maintain balance by keeping prey populations in check, preventing overgrazing and starvation.

In nature, conflict creates balance. Remove the conflict, and the balance falls apart.

4. No Pain, No Survival Instinct

If our bodies couldn't feel pain, we'd never pull our hands away from a fire, never treat an injury, never avoid danger. But here's the catch—if the world were truly perfect, there wouldn't be any danger in the first place.

The very fact that pain is necessary for survival proves that contrast—good and bad, safe and dangerous—is built into the fabric of reality. Pain isn't a problem—it's a messenger. It's what tells us to stop doing something harmful.

So the issue isn't pain itself but the belief that a world without any bad could actually exist. Without pain, life would actually be more dangerous, not less—because it would mean ignoring the reality that contrast is what makes survival possible in the first place.

5. No Weather, No Life

A world with no bad weather—no storms, hurricanes, or floods—sounds appealing until you realize what weather actually does.

- Storms and floods redistribute nutrients, water, and seeds, making sure that life can thrive in new places.
- Even lightning, which seems destructive, helps to fix nitrogen in the soil, making it fertile for plants.

The things we call "bad weather" are part of what keeps the earth alive and evolving.

6. If Nothing Ever Ended, Nothing Would Matter

If no one ever died, no one aged, and you could live however long you wanted, nothing would matter.

- Urgency gives life meaning. Knowing that time is limited is what makes us appreciate sunsets, love deeply, and strive for more.
- If you had infinite time, why pursue anything? Why work for anything, love anyone, or build anything? You could always do it later—forever.

We'd all become professional procrastinators. There would be no reason to do anything now because "later" would stretch on forever.

The limit of time is what makes every moment precious. When you know that time is running out, you live differently—you make the call, take the risk, say "I love you" instead of waiting for the perfect moment that might never come.

A world without endings wouldn't be paradise—it would be a waiting room with no clock.

7. No Challenges, No Growth

Imagine a world with no challenges, no conflicts, no struggles. At first, it sounds like peace. But in reality, it would be a kind of stagnation—no need to grow, learn, or overcome anything.

- Challenges force us to evolve—both as individuals and as a species.
- The most inspiring stories, the deepest love, and the greatest wisdom come from struggle—not from coasting along.

If you remove the mountain, you remove the climb—and the view at the top.

8. Suffering as a Wake-Up Call

Suffering can even wake us up—think of those who've turned pain into wisdom or compassion. It's not "needed," but it's part of the mix.

Like a caterpillar dissolving into mush inside its cocoon, the process looks brutal and hopeless—until it breaks free as a butterfly. In the same way, what feels like the end could just be part of the process that transforms you into something greater.

The point isn't that suffering is good or that we should seek it out. The point is that suffering is part of the contrast that makes life what it is.

- It's not a flaw in the design—it's part of the design.
- Without contrast, there's no experience—only an endless, neutral existence where nothing stands out, nothing matters, and nothing ever changes.

That's why a world without suffering wouldn't be perfect—it would be empty.

At the end of the day, the real question isn't why suffering exists but who is experiencing it. If all beings are expressions of the same consciousness, then every joy and every pain is just life experiencing itself through different forms.

When you realize this, you stop asking, "Why does God allow suffering?" and start asking, "Who is the one that sees the suffering?" And when you trace that question back to its source, you find that it's always been the same one consciousness, experiencing itself in infinite ways.

That's when the whole illusion of opposites starts to dissolve, and you begin to see things as they really are—different waves, same ocean.

THE FLAME THAT NEVER LEFT

Grief is one of the heaviest human experiences—a weight that presses down on the chest, a silence that roars louder than words. No teaching, no philosophy, no well-meaning perspective should rush in to sweep it away. To feel grief is not a failure to overcome: it is a testament to having loved.

This chapter isn't about letting go of that love—it's about seeing it for what it truly is.

Grief: Love in Search of Form

Grief is love in search of form. It's the piercing ache that comes when the physical presence of someone we cherished—their voice, their touch, their familiar shape in the world—slips beyond our reach.

We mourn the body, the tangible vessel, because it's what we could see and hold. But what if that form was never the source of love, only its fleeting expression? The love we feel doesn't vanish when the body does—it lingers, seeking a new way to be known.

The Illusion of Loss

"The illusion of loss begins with the illusion of separateness."

Consider a candle burning brightly in a darkened room. The flame isn't a solitary thing—it's a dance of wax, wick, and air, borrowing its glow from the elements around it.

When the flame flickers out, we say it's "gone," but where did it go? The warmth lingers in the air, the wax has melted into a new shape, the light has touched everything it reached. The flame was never separate from its surroundings: it was a process, a transformation. What we call "extinguished" is just a shift in form.

So it is with those we love. The body may fall away, but what we truly are—what they truly were—cannot be confined to flesh and bone. Consciousness, like fire, cannot be grasped or contained. It dances through life, then changes its shape.

We weep because the dance we knew has ended, but the essence that animated it hasn't departed. They haven't gone "somewhere else." They are right here, woven into the fabric of existence, beyond the veil of what our eyes can see.

Transformation, Not Endings

You've never truly touched your loved one—only their form. What you loved most was their presence, their essence, their awareness. That presence was never separate from your own.

When we lose someone, we don't lose their love—we lose the costume it wore. The essence remains, alive in the quiet spaces of our hearts, in the stillness that follows the storm of tears.

Love, when it is real, doesn't die with the body. It persists in the silence, in the awareness that emerges when the mind grows calm. The pain of grief comes not from love's absence, but from our longing for its familiar shape. Yet that longing itself is proof that love endures.

Grief as a Gateway

Grief can be a gateway—a raw, unyielding force that shatters the ego's illusion of control. It drags us into depths we might never have explored otherwise, stripping away the superficial until we're left face-to-face with what doesn't change.

If we dare to sit with it, to let it wash over us without resistance, grief reveals something profound: the connection we mourn hasn't broken. It's only transformed.

This doesn't mean the pain disappears. It means the pain becomes a teacher, guiding us toward a truth we might have overlooked in happier times: what we truly loved was never limited to the form we lost.

Honoring the Bond

So yes—grieve. Feel it fully. Let the tears come, let the memories flood in, let the weight settle into your bones. Mourn the form, honor the bond—it's yours to carry for as long as you need.

But amidst the sorrow, remember this:

- You don't have to stop missing them.
- You don't have to stop feeling the pain.
- You only have to recognize that what you truly loved never left.

A Moment of Reflection

Take a quiet moment now. Sit with the memory of the one you've lost—not the face, not the voice, but the presence behind it all. Close your eyes and feel for the essence you loved—the warmth, the laughter, the unspoken understanding.

That's what they were to you.

That's what still remains.

Let your grief guide you to it, like a thread leading back to the source.

In that space, beyond the illusion of loss, love breathes on.

THOUGHTS AND EMOTIONS

Your Mind Is Like a Streaming Service

Your mind works a lot like a streaming app. Every thought that shows up is kind of like a recommendation—picked based on what you've paid attention to before. It might feel random sometimes, but it's usually shaped by your past habits, memories, and conditioning.

Thoughts Are Like Suggested Videos or Songs

The mind is constantly throwing out suggestions, some meaningful, some just noise. You don't get to control which thoughts appear—just like you can't control which videos show up on your YouTube homepage. But you do get to choose what you click on. The more you engage with a certain kind of thought, the more your mind serves you similar ones—just like clicking on one type of video brings more of the same. But just because a thought shows up doesn't mean you have to follow it. You're not obligated to click on every suggestion that appears.

Emotions Are Like the Algorithm's Reaction

Here's where it gets interesting. The algorithm on a streaming service reacts based on what you engage with. If you watch a scary video, you'll get more fear-based content. If you listen to a sad song, you'll get more heartbreak playlists. The mind works the same way.

- Click on a fearful thought—your emotions respond with anxiety.
- Click on a nostalgic memory—your emotions respond with longing.
- Click on an empowering thought—your emotions respond with motivation.

Your emotions are just the mind's way of reacting to what you focus on. Change what you click on, and over time, you'll change what the algorithm (your emotions) feeds you.

How Social Media Hacks Your Mind's Algorithm

Ever wonder why you can't stop scrolling on TikTok or YouTube? That's no accident. Social media platforms have mastered this algorithmic game. They keep track of what you pause on, what you like, and what you share. If you keep engaging with conspiracy theories, you'll get more of them. If you watch motivational videos, your feed becomes a self-improvement wonderland.

It's a feedback loop:

- **Fear-based Content:** Keeps you anxious and on high alert.
- **Inspirational Content:** Lifts you up and keeps you striving for more.
- **Controversial Content:** Triggers strong emotions to keep you hooked.

These platforms are essentially playing the same game your mind does. They amplify whatever you give attention to.

Emotional Echo Chambers: How Your Mind Creates Its Own Reality

This creates what's known as an emotional echo chamber—a personalized reality that reflects your emotional patterns back at you. The more you engage with certain types of thoughts or content, the more you believe that's all there is. It's why someone who constantly focuses on negative thoughts starts to see the whole world through a pessimistic lens. It's not the world that's changed—it's the algorithm of your mind.

How This Relates to the Mind?

Your mind is doing the same thing:

- **Thoughts as Clicks:** Every time you focus on a thought—whether it's fearful, joyful, or regretful—you're essentially clicking on it.
- **Emotions as the Algorithm:** Each emotional reaction strengthens the pattern. The more you feel a certain way, the more likely your mind is to revisit those same types of thoughts.
- **Reprogramming the Algorithm:** You can shift the way your mind works by being intentional about which thoughts you give attention to. Over time, this trains your mental patterns to lean toward peace, clarity, and better emotional states.

You can't always control which thoughts or emotions show up—but you do get to choose which ones you feed. The more often you choose wisely, the more your mind starts to reflect that choice—just like how your feed changes based on what you click on.

Breaking the Cycle: Stop Clicking on Negative Content

- **If you keep watching fearful or negative content:** The algorithm (your emotions) will keep feeding you more of it.
- **If you start choosing empowering, calming, or positive content:** The algorithm will shift over time.
- **If you stop engaging with the streaming service entirely (meditation):** The recommendations stop mattering.

It's not about denying emotions but about choosing which ones to amplify.

You're the Platform, Not the Content

- Your mind is not the content—it's the platform that hosts it.
- Your emotions are not permanent—they are just reactions.
- You have the power to change what you engage with and free yourself from the autoplay of unwanted thoughts.

The more you identify with thoughts and emotions, the more turbulent the experience feels. But when you remember what you are—the silent witness behind the stream—it all softens. You don't need to stop the stream. You just need to stop believing it's you.

FISH LOVE VS. TRUE LOVE

Most people think they understand love, but what they call love is often just attachment, comfort, or desire wrapped in poetic words. It isn't love for the other—it's love for what the other provides. That's not divine love. That's what Rabbi Abraham Twerski famously called "Fish Love."

A man says, "I love fish." But what he really means is: "I love the way fish tastes." So he pulls it out of the water, kills it, and eats it. He doesn't love the fish—he loves himself.

Now think of how most people describe love:

"I love how you make me feel."

"I love how you take care of me."

"I love that you make me laugh."

All of these are subtle ways of saying, "I love what you do for me." This is Fish Love. It is not love for the other as they are. It is love for how they serve your sense of self.

But here's the twist: If there is no true "other," is even Fish Love still selfish? If all is One, then all love is ultimately the Self loving itself in another form. Even attachment, even desire, even the most egoic kind of love is still the ocean reaching for itself through its own waves.

In the highest sense, there is no such thing as 'selfish' or 'unselfish,' because both assume the existence of a separate self. And from the view of non-duality, separation is the illusion.

But within the human experience, where the illusion still feels real, these distinctions do matter—because they reveal whether a person is acting from ego or awareness. The key isn't to reject morality but to see where it's arising from.

But that doesn't mean all forms of love are equal.

Fish Love is rooted in ignorance—in the mistaken belief that you lack something, and that someone else can fill that void. It's the ego craving completion.

True Love, on the other hand, arises from realization. It flows not from need, but from wholeness. It sees no separation, no transaction, no dependency. It doesn't say, "I need you." It says, "I see you as Me."

"It is not for the sake of the wife that the wife is loved, but for the sake of the Self that the wife is loved."
—Brihadaranyaka Upanishad 2.4.5

This is not a selfish statement. It is a dissolving of self and other. It means: I recognize that there is no real boundary between what I am and what you are. In loving you, I am loving my own essence.

That's why the highest love isn't found in clinging, needing, or grasping. It's found in freedom. In stillness. In being. It doesn't require effort because it is not manufactured by the mind. It arises naturally when the illusion of separateness dissolves.

So if you want to know if your love is true, ask yourself:

Would I still love them if they stopped doing things that pleased me?

Would I still love them if they changed completely?

Would I still love them if they gave me nothing?

If the answer is yes, not out of obligation, but from presence, then what you have may not be Fish Love. It may be the real thing.

And if you love like that, you are no longer a wave seeking the ocean.

You are the ocean, loving its own reflection.

Why Do You Love Jesus?

After reading about Fish Love and True Love, ask yourself: Why do I love Jesus?

Most people, when asked this question, say things like:

"Because he died for my sins."

"Because he saved me."

"Because he comforts me, protects me, or forgives me."

But look closer. These are all forms of:

"I love what he does for me."

That is Fish Love.

And if you love Jesus only because of what you get from him—then is that love for Jesus? Or is it love for the idea of rescue? Is it love for the Self—or fear of being without a Savior?

When we love Jesus not as an external figure but as a mirror—one who reflected back our own divine essence—then the love becomes pure. We're not adoring a separate being but awakening to the same light within. He didn't come to be worshiped—he came to show us what we are.

Then your love is not egoic—it is Truth Love.

- "I and the Father are one." —John 10:30
- "The Kingdom of God is within you." —Luke 17:21
- "Before Abraham was, I AM." —John 8:58

Jesus wasn't asking to be worshiped. He was inviting people to awaken. To realize the same "I AM" within them. To see through the illusion of separation.

The moment we love Jesus as an image or identity, we risk missing the Truth he was pointing to.

But when we love him as the Self recognizing the Self, the wave seeing the Ocean behind another wave—then we aren't loving a man.

We are loving the One through the One.

So again:

Why do you love Jesus?

Let the question echo—not to shame you, but to wake you up.

JESUS AND NON-DUALITY: "I AND THE FATHER ARE ONE"

In John 10:30, Jesus states, "I and the Father are one." Traditional theology often interprets this as a claim to exclusive divinity, positioning Jesus as the sole Son of God. However, through the lens of non-duality, a more profound understanding emerges—one that transcends exclusivity and points to a universal truth.

In a non-dual view, Jesus' words were not a claim to exclusive divinity, but an expression of the universal truth—that the essence of God resides in all beings. The phrase "I AM" is not an identity limited to Jesus—it is the eternal truth of existence itself. It is not a personal name but the very essence of being, beyond labels, beyond the mind's conditioning.

A lot of people think Jesus came to pay a debt—like humanity owed something so big that only divine blood could settle it. But if that's true, what does it say about God? That He couldn't forgive without payment? That love had a price tag? That's not grace. That's a transaction. Then some people say, "It was a gift—with no attachments."

But that's the contradiction: Forgiveness means letting go of a debt. Payment means satisfying a debt.

You can't have both. It's like student loan forgiveness. If someone pays off your loan, it's still a transaction. But if the loan is canceled—gone, no one pays—that's real forgiveness. So when people say, "Jesus paid our debt" and then call it a free gift—they don't realize they're mixing two opposite ideas. It can't be both a payment and a gift with no strings. From a non-dual perspective, the real problem wasn't sin—it was the belief in separation.

Jesus didn't die to change God's mind about humanity. He came to change humanity's mind about God. That's not a bailout. That's awakening.

Many people believe that we must "accept the gift" of Christ to be saved. And from a certain perspective, that holds deep truth. But in the non-dual understanding, this "acceptance" is less about receiving something external, and more about awakening to what's already within us. Jesus wasn't offering a transaction—he was extending an invitation to remember.

To "accept the gift" is to remember who you truly are in God—not separate, not condemned, but already held in divine wholeness. In that remembrance, the illusion of separation dissolves—and that's what brings liberation.

It's not about earning salvation. It's about waking up to the truth that it was never withheld to begin with.

And the scriptures quietly confirm this:

"To wit, that God was in Christ, reconciling the world unto himself, not imputing their trespasses unto them…" —2 Corinthians 5:19 (KJV)

That doesn't sound like a God collecting payment—it sounds like a God restoring relationship.

And as Romans 6:23 (KJV) says: "For the wages of sin is death; but the gift of God is eternal life through Jesus Christ our Lord."

Notice the contrast: wages are earned, gifts are given. You can't have both.

But here's the deeper truth—one that bridges scripture and realization:

Sin is only experienced in duality. And so is death.

Sin is not the fundamental reason we die. Sin arises from what we perceive as the negative aspects of duality—where there's a 'me' and a 'God,' a 'right' and a 'wrong,' a 'saved' and a 'damned.' And so does birth and death.

These are not eternal truths—they are temporary experiences inside the illusion of separation. From a broader view, we don't truly die—only the form dissolves. The Self never dies because it was never born. That's not philosophy. That's freedom.

For additional scriptures that support the idea of shared divinity, see Appendix D.

The Deeper Context: "Is it not written in your Law, 'I said, you are gods'?" (John 10:34)

Imagine this scenario: Jesus is surrounded by people accusing Him of blasphemy for claiming oneness with God. Instead of denying it or claiming superiority, He reminds them of their own Scriptures, essentially saying:

"If your own texts call you gods because you represent divine authority, why then is it blasphemy for me to say I am one with God? Perhaps you do not understand what it truly means to be a 'god.' It is not about power or status—it is about realizing the oneness with the divine essence that is within all of us."

Oneness, Not Separation

This statement aligns perfectly with Non-Duality teaching that the true Self (Atman) is not separate from the Absolute Reality (Brahman). Jesus wasn't saying, "Only I am divine," but was pointing others back to their own divine nature. He embodied God—but so do you.

Revealing, Not Defending

Rather than defending his own status, Jesus might have been attempting to elevate his audience's understanding. He wasn't trying to escape a blasphemy charge but instead inviting them to see beyond the illusion of separation—that "I and the Father are one" is not an exclusive claim but a universal truth.

BY DAVID ENGLAND

The Spiritual Genius of Jesus' Message

By referencing Psalm 82:6, Jesus:

- Disarmed His Critics: He used their own scriptures to neutralize their accusations.
- Taught Non-Duality: He subtly suggested that divinity is not an external status but an internal realization.
- Exposed Hypocrisy: His accusers, who claimed authority as religious leaders, did not recognize the divine truth even when it was reflected back at them.

Jesus as a Mirror to Higher Truth

When viewed through a Vedantic lens, Jesus' actions and words reflect a profound teaching of oneness. He wasn't simply playing word games to avoid persecution—he was using the mirror of scripture to show his audience their own divine reflection. This approach not only makes his response logically sound but also transforms the entire narrative into a lesson on awakening rather than a defense against blasphemy. It shows Jesus not as a man trying to justify himself but as a master teacher attempting to open eyes to the truth of oneness that lies within all of us.

The "I AM" and the Nature of Divine Oneness

Think about this: When someone asks, "Who are you?", your instinctive response is "I AM"—but you do not stop there. You immediately attach an identity: "I am John," or "I am a teacher," or "I am a father." But before the name, before the roles, before the body, before the mind—there is simply I AM.

That pure awareness, that silent presence before all labels—is your true nature.

Consider when Moses asked God, "Who shall I say sent me?" and the answer was:

"I AM THAT I AM."

Not "God," for that is merely a title or label created by man. Not "I am this" or "I am that," but I AM. No limitation. No form. No separation. Pure, formless existence.

This is the essence of non-duality.

When Jesus said, "Before Abraham was, I AM" (John 8:58), he was not claiming an individual identity but pointing to the eternal presence beyond time. It was not "I, the man, Jesus" who existed before Abraham, but the infinite I AM, which is beyond birth and death. The same I AM that speaks through you, through all beings, through all existence itself.

The Awakening to Your Divine Nature

Jesus' teachings were not merely about himself as a divine exception but about awakening others to their own divine potential:

- "The Kingdom of God is within you." (Luke 17:21) Not in a distant realm, but in the realization of your true nature.
- "Is it not written in your Law, 'I said, you are gods'?" (John 10:34) A direct challenge to the illusion of separation, reminding humanity of their divine essence.

- "Be still and know that I AM God." (Psalm 46:10) Not an instruction to worship, but to awaken to the presence of divinity within.

Jesus was not teaching separation—he was pointing to oneness.

The True Message of Christ

If Jesus were here today, would he want worship—or awakening? Would he desire followers—or realized beings who see as he saw?

He did not teach fear—he taught love.

He did not preach separation—he preached oneness.

He did not come to create a religion—he came to awaken humanity.

The truth of Christ is not found in churches, rituals, or blind faith. It is found in the direct experience of divine unity.

"The Kingdom of God is within you."

The question is: Are you ready to see it?

But if Christ represents the realization of oneness—what, then, represents the resistance to that truth?

The Anti-Christ: The Illusion of the Opposite

If Jesus symbolized the awakened Self—the "I AM" presence that recognizes its oneness with the Source—then the Anti-Christ is not merely a future tyrant or apocalyptic villain. It is the mental construct that opposes that awakening. Not because it is evil but because it clings to identity, division, and separation.

In 1 John 2:18, it says: "Even now many antichrists have come." This wasn't a prophecy—it was an observation. The Anti-Christ isn't a person. It's a pattern of thought—the egoic tendency to reject inner truth and worship outer form. It denies the divine spark within while bowing to authority without. It hides behind religion yet resists revelation. While Christ represents the realization "I and the Father are One," the Anti-Christ clings to "I am only this body, only this mind." One reveals unity; the other insists on separation.

Let's break down the term: Anti-Christ

"Anti" means opposed to or against.

"Christ" comes from the Greek Christos—meaning "the anointed one," a translation of the Hebrew Messiah.

So literally: "Anti-Christ" means opposed to the anointed one.

But here's the question: What does that really mean?

Does it mean that anyone who doesn't accept Jesus as "the Son of God" is an Anti-Christ?

What about Muslims, who honor Jesus as a prophet? What about Hindus, Buddhists, Taoists, or atheists? Are they Anti-Christs just because they don't use the same vocabulary or dogma?

If we take the term at face value, it becomes absurdly exclusive. It implies that billions of people around the world are "against Christ" simply because they don't subscribe to a specific theological framework. But that's not only illogical—it's un-Christlike.

The deeper issue is this:

What does the "Anti-Christ" actually bring that isn't already here?

The world already contains hatred, division, greed, ego, violence, and spiritual ignorance. These aren't future threats—they're present realities. So, if Anti-Christ means opposing the anointed path, then many who claim Christ are also walking in opposition to him.

If you say you follow Christ but your heart is closed, your words are harsh, and your love is conditional—what spirit are you really following?

As I always say:

Your audio needs to match your video.

Belief without action is just noise.

True Christ-likeness means loving not just the ones who agree with you, but the ones who challenge you.

Living Christ or Living Anti-Christ

So perhaps we need to rethink this entire concept—not as a person to fear but as a principle to recognize. Every time we act from ego instead of love, from separation instead of unity, we step into Anti-Christ consciousness. And every moment we return to stillness, kindness, and truth—we embody the anointed path.

Being Christlike is not about reciting the right scriptures. It's about living from the truth within you.

And the real question isn't, "Who is the Anti-Christ?" The real question is: In this moment, am I reflecting the Christ within me—or resisting it?

So don't look for the Anti-Christ in world leaders or conspiracy theories. Look in the mirror. Look in your reactions. The real battle isn't out there. It's within you.

And the victory? It's not won with swords or scripture. It's won with awareness.

THE FIVE DOORS AND THE ONE WHO SEES

How the Senses Shape Our World

Ever wonder what "the world" would be if you'd never tasted sweetness, heard a sound, or seen a single color? It's tough to even imagine, right? Everything we know—every tree, every breeze, every bite of food—comes through five little doorways: sight, sound, touch, taste, and smell. They're like instruments we use to piece together what we call "reality."

Think about it: you don't really *see* the world—just colors and shapes your eyes catch. You don't *hear* it—just vibrations your brain turns into meaning. Same with touch, taste, smell—each one's a filter, giving you a slice of what's out there. But here's a wild question: if all those senses vanished, would the world still exist for you?

And here's where it gets interesting—something's catching all these sights and sounds. Let's explore what that is. We'll take a little stroll together, sense by sense, and see what we find.

The Inquiry – Peeling Back the Senses

Grab a comfy spot, maybe close your eyes if you feel like it. No pressure here—we're just taking a peek at what's always been there, seeing what sticks around when the usual stuff fades out.

1. Sight – "What's here without seeing?"

Shut your eyes for a sec. No colors, no shapes, no sense of "out there." The room fades away—but does the one noticing it vanish too?

- Ask yourself: "Without sight, what's left of the world?"
- "The picture's gone—am I still here?"
- Take a breath. Notice: you're still around. The *seen* drops, but the *seer* doesn't.

2. Sound – "Who's here in silence?"

Now, let sound drift to the background. Don't worry about blocking noise—just tune into the quiet underneath. If no sound popped up, would you disappear? Or would you just be aware of the stillness?

- "If silence takes over, am I still here?"
- You're not the ear—you're what knows what the ear picks up.

3. Touch – "What am I without sensation?"

Feel the seat under you, the air on your skin. Now picture those feelings melting away, like snow in the sun—no texture, no temperature, no edges. If touch faded, would you vanish?

- "No signals from the body—am I still present?"
- You're not the sensations—you're what notices them.

4. Smell – "What's left without scent?"

Notice your nose, the air. Then imagine no smell at all—just a blank slate. Does that change who you are?

- "No scent—does awareness fade too?"
- Nope. It's still here, untouched.

5. Taste – "Am I here without flavor?"

Let your tongue rest. No sweetness, no salt. If taste disappeared, what happens?

- "No flavor—am I gone?"
- Nothing changes. You're still you.

What's Left?

So, we've peeled back all five: no sight, no sound, no touch, no smell, no taste. And yet—you're still here. You haven't disappeared. You're still aware—just without the layers.

Here's the big reveal: you're not what you perceive. You're the one who perceives. After dropping each sense, what's still here? Not the sights or sounds but the awareness that saw them all along. Think of the senses as waves on the ocean—they come and go, but you're the ocean itself, always there, with or without the splash.

The Final Question

Now, here's the fun part: what's aware of all this? Don't try to figure it out—just look, like a kid seeing the world for the first time. Let yourself settle into the quiet that's always there, behind it all. It's not a thought—it's who you are. Rest there, not as some big concept, but as the simple truth of you.

Closing Insight

The world shows up through your senses, but when they go quiet, you don't vanish. That flips everything: You're not inside the world—the world appears inside you. And this "you" isn't the body or the mind—it's pure awareness, always here, no matter what's going on. This awareness isn't something you own—it's what you are, plain and simple.

THE PRACTICE OF
SELF-INQUIRY

The moment you stop and really pay attention, you'll notice something profound: everything you think of as "you" is actually something you can observe.

- You can observe your thoughts, so you are not your thoughts.
- You can observe your emotions, so you are not your emotions.
- You can observe your body, so you are not your body.

So if you're not those things, what are you? What remains? The observer itself—pure Awareness.

The mistake is believing that you are what you observe rather than the awareness in which the observation occurs. But can your hand observe itself? Can the eyes see themselves? Can the mind know the knower? The moment you realize that everything you perceive—including thoughts—are objects appearing *to* awareness, the illusion that you are those objects begins to dissolve.

Thoughts appear and disappear, but you remain. The mind can be observed, just like clouds drifting across the sky. If you can see something, you are not it. So, who is the one aware of the mind?

Self-Inquiry Exercises

If you really want to experience this truth for yourself, don't just read it—practice it. The following exercises will help you uncover the reality of who you are. Try each one slowly, giving yourself time to truly reflect.

Preparation

Before beginning these exercises, take a moment to strip away everything you think you are. Close your eyes. For a few minutes, let go of your name. Let go of your job, your past, your beliefs, your ambitions, your roles, your story, your values—even your spiritual identity. Let go of all the things you associate with being "you." Imagine you had never been told who you are, what you believe, or what your role is in this world.

Now, ask yourself one simple question: Who am I?

If everything you call "yourself" is stripped away, what remains?

Rethinking the Soul

Some may respond, ***"I am the soul that God gave."***

But let's pause.

Genesis doesn't say "God gave man a soul."

It says: **"Man became a living soul."**

So the soul is not a possession—it is an expression of being.

Still, even the concept of a "soul" is something you can be aware of.

So the deeper question becomes:

> *What is aware of the soul?*
> *If the soul is something you can think about, reflect on, or feel connection to, then there's something even more fundamental than it.*

Even the idea of the soul is something you can notice—something you're aware of. But if you can observe it, then you must be something deeper.

You're not the thought of a soul, or a person with a soul—you're the awareness that sees it all. That quiet presence behind every experience—that's the real you.

Does the soul come and go?

- If the soul appears and disappears, what remains constant?
- That unchanging presence is who you really are—not something that was given or taken.

If you can observe or be aware of the "soul" as a concept, feeling, or subtle experience, then you are not the soul—you are the awareness in which even the soul appears.

Exercise 1: The Watcher of Thoughts

- Close your eyes and sit in silence.
- Observe your thoughts as they arise—don't judge them, don't stop them, just watch.
- Now ask yourself: If I can see these thoughts, who is watching?
- Stay with that question. Try to shift your attention from the thoughts to the awareness that sees them.

Realization: Thoughts come and go, but the one observing them is always there. **You are not the thoughts—you are the awareness behind them.**

Exercise 2: Can You Find Yourself?

- Ask yourself: Where am I?
- You might point to your body, but pause—are you the body, or do you have a body?
- Shift to your mind—are you your thoughts, or do thoughts simply appear to you?
- Keep looking. Whatever you find, ask yourself: Am I observing this? If I can observe it, then it's not me.

Realization: Everything you call "you" is actually something appearing to you. But the real "you" can't be found as an object—it's the awareness in which all objects appear.

Exercise 3: The Vanishing World

- Look around the room you're in. Take in all the details.
- Now, close your eyes. Where did the room go?
- Open them again—it's back. But where did it actually go?
- Realize that the world only appears when it is experienced—without awareness, the world is nothing.

Realization: The universe exists only when experienced—but what is always present, never disappearing? Awareness itself.

All of this leads to a deeper realization—awareness is like a mirror.

- If you see a person in a mirror, can you touch them? **No, you are only touching glass.**
- If there is a fire in the mirror, does the mirror get hot? **No, The fire is only an image.**
- If a storm rages in the mirror, does the mirror break? **No, the storm is only an appearance, not substance.**

Now, apply this to your experience:

- The **body appears** in awareness, but it does not define awareness.
- The **mind appears** in awareness, but it does not limit awareness.
- The **world appears** in awareness, but it does not change awareness.

The mirror analogy reveals a powerful truth: You are not the person inside the mirror—you are the mirror itself. The reflections come and go, but the mirror remains unchanged. The same way reflections appear in the mirror without altering it, the universe appears in consciousness without changing what you really are.

When you see a car in your rear view mirror, is there actually a car inside? No, only glass.

Likewise, when you experience the universe, is there actually a separate, external world? No, there is only consciousness appearing as a world.

- You are not in the universe—the universe is in You.
- You are not affected by the world—the world is a dream appearing in You.
- You are not separate from anything—there is only One Reality, Awareness.

When this realization dawns, suffering dissolves, and only peace remains. The reflections will continue to dance, but the mirror will always be still. You are that mirror—unshaken, untouched, infinite.

Stan Lee and Spider-Man Analogy

Stan Lee created Spider-Man—but he didn't become Spider-Man. He imagined him into existence, gave him thoughts, emotions, a story, and a world. Every word Spider-Man says, every challenge he faces, every villain he fights—it's all coming from Stan Lee's mind.

But here's the catch: even though Stan Lee created Spider-Man, Spider-Man is not separate from Stan Lee. He's a projection of Stan's imagination—yet within the story, Spider-Man seems like an independent, heroic person with his own identity and choices.

In the same way, God didn't become creation—but everything in creation is an expression of God's consciousness. You, me, the world—we're all "characters" in the divine mind. And the moment we forget the author, we believe we're just the character.

> *Ancient Echo: The Web and the Self*
> "As a spider spins its web from itself and withdraws it back into itself,
> so does the universe emerge from Brahman and return to Brahman."
> — *Mundaka Upanishad*

This entire reality, with all its names and forms, arises from the Self, dances for a time, and returns to the Self.

Your role in the play is not accidental—it's divine.

But never forget: you are not the story.

You are the awareness in which the story appears.

THE SYMBOL OF EVERYTHING

O + ∑ = ∞ | 1 + 7 = 8 — A Symbolic Revelation
My Discovery

Some discoveries arrive through years of research and analysis. Others emerge suddenly, like a flash of lightning in a dark sky. The equation (O + ∑ = ∞) — or as expressed numerically, "1 + 7 = 8" — was the latter. It didn't arise from complex mathematics or scientific theory, but from stillness—from deep contemplation and meditation. It surfaced not from intellect, but from something deeper—an intuitive knowing beyond the mind.

The number 8 had always fascinated me. Its form, an endless loop without beginning or end, symbolizes infinity (∞). It represents balance, the eternal flow of existence, and the resolution of duality into unity. The more I contemplated it, the more I realized that 8 was more than a number—it was the symbol of everything.

But how could one arrive at 8 without complex equations, especially for someone who isn't a mathematician? I decided to work backwards.

BY DAVID ENGLAND

"If 8 is the symbol of everything," I thought, "then how do we arrive at it?"

I started with 1—the most fundamental of all numbers. In Non-Duality philosophy, 1 represents Oneness—the ultimate, indivisible reality from which everything emerges. The word "unit" itself is derived from 1, symbolizing unity and the source of all things. If 1 is Oneness, then what could bridge the gap between the one and the infinite (8)?

That's when it came to me: The universe, as it appears to us, unfolds according to principles—movements of the One appearing as the many. These laws were not arbitrary but essential truths woven into the fabric of reality. And in the Hermetic tradition, these laws were encapsulated in the 7 Hermetic Principles: Mentalism, Correspondence, Vibration, Polarity, Rhythm, Cause and Effect, and Gender.

1 (Oneness) + 7 (The Hermetic Principles) = 8 (Infinity).

The simplicity of this equation was staggering. In a single line, it encapsulated the journey of existence:

- 1: The source, Oneness, the undivided whole.
- 7: The principles that govern the manifestation of reality.
- 8: The infinite nature of existence, the resolution of duality into unity.

This wasn't just a mathematical insight—it was a spiritual revelation. The equation wasn't a matter of numbers but of symbols, each representing an aspect of the journey from unity, through the multiplicity of universal laws, back to unity. It was a way of expressing how the many emerge from the One and return to the One, all without losing their essence.

The Symbolism of 8

Why was I so fascinated with the number 8? It was more than the way it looked on paper. The form of 8, turned sideways, becomes the symbol of infinity (∞)—a flow without end, a reminder that all beginnings are endings, and all endings are beginnings. It represents a cosmic balance, a state where opposites do not cancel each other but complete each other.

- In Chinese philosophy, 8 is considered the number of balance and harmony.
- In Kabbalah, the 8th sphere represents glory and eternity.
- In mathematics, it is a number of perfect symmetry.

In essence, 8 is the ultimate reminder that what appears as two (the loops of 8) is actually one—a continuous flow of existence that has neither start nor finish. This is why $1 + 7 = 8$ is so profound. It isn't just an equation; it's a map of existence. It's duality wrapped into unity—a symbol where opposites dance within a single, flowing form.

1: Oneness – The Starting Point

The equation begins with 1 because all things originate from the source, the undivided consciousness that Vedanta refers to as Brahman. In the physical world, we see multiplicity—countless forms and phenomena. But from the highest perspective, all are expressions of the same source.

This idea challenges the illusion of separation that governs most of human perception. The number 1 symbolizes the realization that beneath all the differences lies a single, unbroken reality.

BY DAVID ENGLAND

7: The Hermetic Principles – The Laws of Manifestation

The 7 Hermetic Principles act as the bridge between Oneness and Infinity. They describe how the One expresses itself through the many:

- **Mentalism:** The universe is a mental construct within the mind of the One.
- **Correspondence:** The macrocosm reflects the microcosm.
- **Vibration:** Everything is in constant motion.
- **Polarity:** Opposites are not truly separate—they are the same in essence, differing only by degree.
- **Rhythm:** The universe moves in cycles.
- **Cause and Effect:** Nothing happens by chance.
- **Gender:** Creative forces exist in everything.

These principles are the mechanics of manifestation—the rules by which the One plays the game of existence. Without them, the infinite potential of the One would remain unexpressed, a blank canvas without form or color.

8: Infinity – The Return to Unity

At the end of this journey is 8, the symbol of infinity. This number signifies the resolution of duality into unity:

The two loops of 8 represent the apparent duality—light and dark, good and evil, self and other.

The continuous flow of the shape symbolizes the eternal cycle of existence, where opposites do not cancel but complement each other.

Infinity is not a destination but a recognition: the realization that what appears as many is truly One. Just as a river flowing into the ocean becomes indistinguishable from it, all individual expressions return to the source without losing their essence.

Conclusion: The Symbol of Everything

In the end, "1 + 7 = 8" is more than an equation. It is a revelation of how the universe operates:

1: Oneness is the source.

7: The principles are the process.

8: Infinity is the realization.

This equation shows that duality is not the opposite of unity but its expression. It reveals that the journey from oneness through the laws of the universe to infinity is not a linear path but a circle—or more accurately, an infinite loop.

To understand this is to see beyond the illusion of separation, to awaken to the truth that all is one. And in this realization lies the key to freedom, the answer to the mystery of existence, and the end of the search.

"1 + 7 = 8"—the symbol of everything.

THE THIRD THAT FORGOT
THE WHOLE

A Fraction with a Hidden Truth

One-third. Just a fraction, right? A simple division of a whole into three parts. On paper, it looks clean, manageable—a math class basic. But stare at it long enough, and it starts to behave strangely. Divide 1 by 3 and what do you get? 0.333… repeating forever. A number that never resolves. A decimal that never becomes whole. It keeps trying, but never arrives. That number? It's a lie dressed like truth. A glitch in the illusion. It points to something deeper than math—a truth about illusion, repetition, and forgetting.

What if this isn't just arithmetic? What if it's a mirror of our own condition? A symbol of the mind that sees itself as a part, forgetting it came from the Whole? What if we, too, are the third that forgot the circle we came from?

The Circle and the Cut

Before there was three, there was One. The undivided. The circle. The Whole. From that Whole came division. Not real division—but perceived fragmentation. Like slicing a pie and mistaking the slice for the meal, we began to identify with the part instead of the whole.

A third isn't wrong. It's not evil. But it's incomplete. And when it believes it is the full picture, it begins to repeat itself endlessly. Just like 0.333…

The ego is the part that believes it is separate. It doesn't know it's the Whole playing as a part. It forgets the circle it came from. And so it keeps seeking, repeating, striving—forever chasing the wholeness it already is.

One-Third of Heaven Fell

The Bible says a third of the angels fell from heaven (Revelation 12:4). Tradition paints this as rebellion. A celestial mutiny. Lucifer and his followers cast out for pride and ambition.

But look deeper.

Can a perfect being fall? Can something in the presence of pure divinity choose separation unless it forgets its source? And if God is truly infinite, can anything truly stand apart from Him?

From a non-dual lens, the fall of angels isn't a war story. It's a symbol. The angels that "fell" represent awareness identifying with form. With individuality. With ego. They're not malevolent spirits at odds with God—they're fragments of the Whole convinced they've become separate. They are expressions of the One caught in illusion, mistaking a ripple for the ocean.

They are the third that forgot the Whole.

Mind, Body, Soul: The Illusion of Three

We're told we're made of three parts: mind, body, and soul. Some say spirit, soul, and flesh. Even God is described as a Trinity: Father, Son, Holy Spirit.

But are these really three? Or are they one thing seen through three lenses? Three words for the same light bouncing through different prisms?

Non-duality doesn't deny the experience of form. It just points past it. The mind isn't separate from the body. The soul isn't floating off in some corner of heaven. All of it—you—is One. Just waves rising and falling on the same ocean. Fingers from the same hand.

The illusion begins the moment we identify with just one part.

"I am the body." "I am my thoughts." "I am my spirit." Those statements sound nice. But each one is a slice talking like it's the pie.

The Ego's Loop in Numbers

The Decimal That Never Ends

0.333…

It looks stable. But it never arrives.

What I mean by "never arrives" is this: mathematically, that decimal repeats forever. You can keep adding 3s infinitely, but it will never reach 1.

You'll go from 3… to 6… to 9… to 12 (1+2 = 3), to 15 (1+5 = 6), to 18 (1+8 = 9), to 21 (2+1 = 3)… and so on. The cycle never breaks. It just keeps orbiting the same pattern.

You might be thinking, "Okay, but what's that got to do with anything?"

Symbolically—it's the **ego**.

That's Samsara. That's the loop. The cycle of seeking, suffering, striving. Always chasing completion. Always feeling "almost there." It's the illusion of being nearly whole.

The ego keeps circling, reincarnating, repeating—thinking, "If I just do more, have more, know more, I'll finally be complete."

But a third can't complete itself. It's stuck in the loop. Until it remembers: it was never three to begin with. It was always One—appearing as three for the experience.

The Problem with Literal Rebellion

Some people double down on the idea that the fall of angels was a literal rebellion—like some divine soap opera. But that story creates more problems than it solves. If heaven is perfect, how does imperfection show up? If God is all, how does something stand outside Him? See the issue?

Dualism needs a villain. A rival. A challenger. But non-duality has no room for that. There's no enemy in the mirror—just a face forgetting it's looking at itself. Lucifer didn't fall. Consciousness didn't "want" to taste form, because Pure Consciousness lacks nothing and wants for nothing. There was no desire. No goal. It didn't dip into illusion to gain—it simply dreamed, spontaneously. Just as humans dream without control, Consciousness dreams reality into motion. No agenda. No plan. Just the mystery of being watching itself move. It dreamed the play. And in that dream, it forgot it was the light.

How Laws Emerge Without a Planner

It doesn't have to create the laws. Because the moment duality manifests, distinction arises. And the moment you have distinction, you have relation. A point A and a point B. A here and a there. That gap—that space between two—is what gives rise to time, form, and motion. And where there is motion, gravity unfolds. Rhythm appears. Correspondence kicks in. Polarity balances.

The laws aren't rules Consciousness wrote—they're the natural ripple effect of division playing itself out. Just like in a dream, where the moment a scene appears, gravity and logic follow—so too in Maya.

Consciousness doesn't author the rules. It simply is, and the dream organizes itself in patterned logic once the illusion of form takes root. The laws emerge within the illusion—not outside it.

The Third That Forgets

We are all the third. Each of us, thinking we're just a name. Just a role. Just a slice of being. We build whole identities around fragments and forget the formless ocean that birthed them. But that forgetting? That's not a flaw. That's the design. The Divine pretending to be limited so it can remember itself again. Awakening isn't about becoming more. It's about remembering you were never less.

The Circle Was Never Broken.

We say we want to return to God. To Source. But here's the truth:

You never left.

You just blinked.

The third was never thrown out.

It just started looking outward, and in doing so, forgot its true nature.

You were never 0.333...

You are 1

You are the circle

You are the Whole

And the moment you remember that...

The illusion ends.

And if you haven't already... take another look at the cover. See if you can spot the illusion now. It's been in front of you the whole time.

AFTERWORD:
WHEN AWAKENING HURTS

I used to think awakening meant becoming detached—like I had to stop loving this world in order to see through it. But that's not how it happened. I saw through the illusion... and I cried like a baby first born into the world. Not because it was real in the ultimate sense, but because it was so beautiful, even in its impermanence.

I realized I might never hold my children again as this person. I might never hear my wife's laughter in this same tone, from this same body. And though I knew none of it was ever truly mine, the grief came like a wave. Because I had loved the dream deeply.

But in that grief, something whispered:

"What you loved was never the form. It was the Light shining through it."

And that Light... is never gone.

It only changes clothes.

Now I understand why humanity created so many comforting after-life theories—to soften the pain of realizing this life, as we know it, will end. This realization can be disturbing when it lands deep. From the ultimate view, it's not so different from how we see an ant's life: one disappears, another takes its place. Existence continues. New identities appear. New experiences unfold. The Atman—pure witnessing Awareness—remains untouched, watching the play.

And one day, another "you" will rise in this play. But it won't remember this version. It will be just as fresh, just as intimate, as this life feels now.

New people. New things to love and to resist.

It's beautiful—but also gut-wrenching when we're attached to the illusion.

And most of us are… including myself.

But now, we're aware of it—and that matters.

So love and cherish this life fully.

Because this one will not be repeated with the same cast.

Thank you for taking the time to hear my voice in this sea of voices.

I truly appreciate the love—and I hope you found something meaningful in these pages.

With love,

David

ACKNOWLEDGMENTS

This book is the result of deep inquiry, years of unlearning, and countless moments of stillness where the mind gave way to something greater. I didn't write this book alone—because truth doesn't belong to one person. It's remembered through many voices, many paths, and many moments of grace.

These words came through me, but not from me. The truths within them were carried by many before me—and will echo in many after.

I wish to acknowledge the wisdom traditions that helped shape the message of this book—especially Advaita Vedanta, Christian mysticism, and the works of Alan Watts, Nisargadatta Maharaj, and Swami Sarvapriyananda. Their words reminded me of what I already knew but had forgotten.

To my family—thank you for your patience, love, and grounding presence. You've been the silent support behind every page.

To those who questioned, challenged, or misunderstood me—thank you, too. Without contrast, clarity cannot arise. Without resistance, realization doesn't deepen.

And to the Source itself—the timeless, wordless Presence from which all this flows—thank you for letting this book pass through me.

May these words serve as a mirror, a nudge, or a spark for those ready to see through the illusion and return to what they've always been.

— David England

MY JOURNEY

I was raised in the Church of Christ and Church of God, later spending years in a Southern Baptist church, searching for something that never fully resonated with me. I questioned everything—Why do I believe this? How does this make sense? If God loves me more than my parents, would He really torture me forever for not following a set of rules?

Those questions sent me spiraling. All I ever felt from religion was fear and sadness. As a teenager, I remember thinking: I may be tortured forever if I don't figure out the right religion—and I didn't even ask to be here.

In my early twenties, I joined the Seventh-Day Adventist Church and followed Doug Batchelor—a brilliant man I still admire to this day. But conditioned beliefs are powerful. If you're not careful, they'll trap you in a box and call it truth. So, my search continued.

I then met a man from India who shook my entire foundation. He recommended *I Am That* by Nisargadatta Maharaj—but I didn't understand it. When I told him, he smirked, 'Ah, you're not ready yet. Read this first, then go back.' He recommended *The Way of the*

Wizard by Deepak Chopra instead. I rolled my eyes, expecting more confusion—but I gave it a shot. To my surprise, it opened a door I didn't know was there.

I started meditating and studying daily—I became obsessed. Slowly, the way I saw the world began to shift. A coworker introduced me to *The Kybalion*, which completely reframed my understanding of reality.

Then an older gentleman—one of the wisest people I've ever met—introduced me to Stoicism and *Way of the Peaceful Warrior* by Dan Millman. His words left a lasting imprint, reshaping how I viewed life, consciousness, and self-awareness. I began to realize that people, circumstances, events—even obstacles—arrive precisely when they're meant to. There are no coincidences.

In the end, it was the teachings of Swami Sarvapriyananda that brought everything full circle. His clarity, depth, and ability to articulate non-duality in a way that pierced through confusion guided me to a truth I had been circling for years. I admire that man deeply. Though he doesn't know me, he helped awaken something in me that no one else could.

Over time, I came to realize there is so much more to God, life, and existence than I ever imagined. Have you ever rewatched a movie and suddenly noticed things you missed the first time? That's exactly what happened. I rewatched the movie of my life—but this time, with clarity instead of confusion.

I didn't get here by blindly accepting what I was told. I learned to question everything—beliefs, assumptions, even the nature of self. I began practicing self-inquiry, stepping back from the noise of the world to observe in stillness. Meditation wasn't just silence—it was a revelation. In that silence, I began to catch glimpses of something deeper... the God within. These weren't just ideas I inherited—they were truths I uncovered through experience, reflection, and a refusal to settle for secondhand answers.

Along the way, I met people—teachers, friends, strangers—who felt like guides placed in my path. Every time I stumbled or felt lost, someone would appear, offering just the piece I needed to continue. They didn't walk the journey for me, but they helped me see what I couldn't yet see on my own. In many ways, they were like mirrors—each reflecting a part of the truth I was searching for. But it was my own questioning, my own seeking, that kept me moving forward.

I'm beyond grateful for this journey. For years, I searched for something I already had within me. I've never felt so deeply connected with God as I do now.

> *I don't believe in God. I rest in God.*
> *Life is beautiful. Life is whole.*
> *Find your balance. Be fully present.*
> *And never stop questioning—because the truth never fears the question.*

The whole meaning of life comes down to one word—Realization.

You are playing a game of hide and seek with yourself.

Are you winning?

APPENDIX

In the following appendices, we'll address specific scriptures and objections for readers interested in deeper clarification and context.

Appendix A:
Scriptural Clarifications for "The Trees of Eden"

This appendix provides a deeper look at key verses used in the chapter *"The Trees of Eden — The Birth of Duality"* to clarify their meanings and address potential misinterpretations from a literalist or dualistic perspective. These clarifications are not meant to dispute scripture but to offer a broader interpretive lens aligned with non-dual philosophy.

1. Genesis 2:17

> "But of the tree of the knowledge of good and evil, thou shalt not eat of it: for in the day that thou eatest thereof thou shalt surely die."

Literal Reading: Implies an immediate, physical death as punishment.

Clarification: Adam and Eve do *not* die physically that day. Instead, their awareness shifts. They "die" to unconscious unity — the seamless oneness of Eden — and awaken into duality and ego. This interpretation aligns with the non-dual idea of "spiritual death": the loss of direct being, replaced by the illusion of separation (the "I" thought).

2. Genesis 3:1

"Now the serpent was more cunning than any beast of the field which the Lord God had made."

Literal Reading: Many assume this is Satan in disguise.

Clarification: The text never mentions Satan. It simply says the serpent is cunning. In non-dual terms, the serpent symbolizes the emerging ego — the first whisper of contrast. It introduces awareness of difference, not evil. The connection to Satan is imposed by later tradition, not the original text.

3. Genesis 3:5

"For God doth know that in the day ye eat thereof, then your eyes shall be opened, and ye shall be as gods, knowing good and evil."

Literal Reading: This is often framed as the serpent lying.

Clarification: This statement proves true in Genesis 3:22 (see below). The serpent's claim is not false — it is fulfilled. What's introduced is not evil, but contrast — knowledge of opposites. This mirrors the awakening of the ego and the illusion of lack.

4. Genesis 3:7

> "And the eyes of them both were opened, and they knew that they were naked; and they sewed fig leaves together, and made themselves aprons."

Literal Reading: The moment of guilt and shame.

Clarification: This verse confirms that *awareness* of duality begins *after* the bite. Their "eyes opening" means they begin to perceive themselves as separate. Nakedness becomes a source of shame — not because of sin, but because of identification with form. This is the birth of ego-consciousness.

5. Genesis 3:22

> "And the Lord God said, Behold, the man is become as one of us, to know good and evil: and now, lest he put forth his hand, and take also of the tree of life, and eat, and live forever..."

Literal Reading: God confirms the change in Adam and Eve.

Clarification: This verse supports the serpent's earlier claim in 3:5 — that their eyes would be opened and they would become "as gods." It also implies they were *not* immortal before the fall. What changes is not their physicality, but their state of consciousness. Now that they "know" good and evil, they can no longer live in unconscious eternity.

6. Genesis 3:24

"So he drove out the man; and he placed at the east of the garden of Eden Cherubims, and a flaming sword which turned every way, to keep the way of the tree of life."

Literal Reading: God bars reentry to Eden.

Clarification: The Tree of Life is not destroyed — only hidden. The "flaming sword" and "cherubims" symbolize the mind's defense mechanisms: once ego arises, direct access to unity is obscured. You cannot return to Eden through effort or control — only through inner stillness and the dissolution of separation.

Conclusion: These verses, when seen through the lens of non-duality, reveal a shift not in morality but in perception. The "fall" is not a crime, but the beginning of self-awareness. The story is not about disobedience, but about awakening — and the cost of that awakening is the illusion of separateness from the Whole.

Appendix B:
Objection-Response Breakdown

This appendix addresses common objections that may arise from readers with a literalist or dualistic interpretation of Genesis. Each response is designed to reinforce the non-dual lens presented in the chapter "The Trees of Eden — The Birth of Duality" while honoring the reader's curiosity and maintaining clarity.

Objection 1: "Eve repeated the command. Doesn't that mean she understood it?"

Response: Repeating a rule is not the same as comprehending its moral implications. Children can mimic phrases like "Don't touch that" without understanding why. Genesis 3:7 confirms that their eyes were opened *after* eating the fruit. This indicates a shift in consciousness that had not yet occurred when Eve quoted the command. She knew the words — not the weight of their meaning.

Objection 2: "This makes it sound like God set them up. Are you saying God caused the fall?"

Response: Not a setup — a setup *for awakening*. The serpent is not a villain who snuck into paradise; it is part of the Whole. In non-dual understanding, contrast arises within unity to allow experience. The Tree of Knowledge is not a trap, but a threshold. God did not *cause* the fall — the story depicts how consciousness awakens through contrast. It is a mythic map, not a courtroom drama.

Objection 3: "You're interpreting the Bible however you want."

Response: Interpretation is inevitable — even literalism is an interpretation. This reading doesn't twist scripture; it respects the original text while offering a broader lens. For example, Genesis never calls the serpent Satan, and the promise in 3:5 comes true in 3:22. These are not reinterpretations — they are honest readings through the lens of inner transformation, not external blame.

Objection 4: "The serpent lied. That means it was evil."

Response: Genesis 3:5 — *"Ye shall be as gods, knowing good and evil"* — is echoed in Genesis 3:22 — *"Behold, the man is become as one of us, to know good and evil."* The serpent didn't lie — it revealed what duality would bring. What it didn't mention was the loss of unity. That's not deception — that's the nature of awakening. The serpent introduced contrast, not corruption.

Objection 5: "You're downplaying sin."

Response: Not at all. This view re-frames sin not as disobedience to a command, but as identification with separation — the moment we forget our true nature. The Bible says they were ashamed after their eyes were opened, not before. This shows sin is not the act of eating but the birth of the illusion of being separate from the Whole.

Objection 6: "You're calling the serpent a good thing. Isn't that dangerous?"

Response: The serpent is not "good" or "evil" — it is the whisper of awareness beginning to differentiate. Just as fire can burn or warm, the ego can lead to suffering or awakening, depending on how it is seen. The serpent is a metaphor for the arising of contrast — not a character to idolize or fear.

Objection 7: "If the serpent isn't Satan, then where did evil come from?"

Response: From the perspective of non-duality, evil is not a force — it's a degree of separation from truth. Just as cold is not a substance but the absence of heat, what we call evil is the forgetting of unity. The serpent doesn't *cause* evil — it introduces awareness of difference, which allows ego to form. Ego isn't evil — but when misidentified with, it becomes the root of suffering.

Objection 8: "You're ignoring God's punishment. The curses are clear."

Response: The curses are descriptive, not necessarily prescriptive. They reveal the natural consequence of seeing through duality. Once the ego arises, contrast is inevitable: pain in childbirth, toil in labor, fear of death. These are not divine punishments — they are the ripple effects of perceiving separation. God is not wrathful — God is witnessing the birth of experience.

Final Note:

This appendix is not meant to silence disagreement but to deepen understanding. The Eden story is not diminished by this lens — it is expanded. It becomes not the story of a mistake, but of awakening — the moment awareness takes form, and the divine forgets itself in order to remember.

Truth doesn't fear questions. It welcomes them.

Appendix C:
Non-Dual Interpretive Keys

This appendix offers simple, grounded explanations of key terms and concepts used in "The Trees of Eden — The Birth of Duality" for readers unfamiliar with non-duality, Advaita Vedanta, or the symbolic language woven throughout the book. These interpretive keys ensure clarity without requiring prior philosophical study.

1. What Is Non-Duality?

Non-duality (Advaita) is the understanding that all of existence is one indivisible reality. There are no separate things — only the appearance of separation. What we call the world, the self, and even God are not three things, but different expressions of the same One.

In this view, the sense of being a separate self ("me") is an illusion created by the mind. The truth is: you are not *in* life, you *are* life — pure awareness appearing as form.

2. What Is the Ego?

The ego is not a villain or a devil — it's simply the false sense of being a separate "I." It is the mental identity we create through thoughts, memory, roles, and beliefs. In Eden, the ego arises the moment Adam and Eve begin to see themselves as separate, as naked, as ashamed. That's the "I" thought being born. The serpent symbolizes this arising — not evil, but awareness differentiating itself into parts.

3. What Is Maya?

Maya is a Sanskrit term meaning illusion — specifically, the illusion that things are separate and that we are limited beings. In Eden,

Maya appears when Adam and Eve believe they must eat the fruit to become more, when in truth they were already whole.

Maya convinces us that we lack something, need something, or must become something to be fulfilled. It's the illusion that hides the truth of our already-perfect nature.

4. What Is Atman?

Atman's the real you—not your body or your thoughts, but the quiet awareness watching it all. It's the divine spark inside, not just yours but the same in everyone. In Advaita, it's one with Brahman—the infinite reality you already are.

5. What Is Brahman?

Brahman is the ultimate reality, the supreme, universal spirit, and the divine essence of the universe, often described as the source, foundation, and goal of all existence.

6. What Is Avidya?

Avidya means spiritual ignorance—the false idea that you are just a body, a mind, or a separate person. It's what makes you forget your true nature. Avidya hides the truth of who you really are: pure, limitless awareness. It's the root cause of suffering and keeps the cycle of karma and rebirth going until you wake up and see clearly.

7. What Is Awareness?

Awareness is not something you have—it's what you are. Before thoughts, before identity, before desire—you are aware. That awareness is constant. Thoughts appear within it, but it remains untouched.

In Advaita, awareness and consciousness point to the same truth: your real Self. Some describe awareness as how consciousness reflects in the mind—but both reveal the unchanging witness within you.

In the Eden story, the Tree of Life represents this pure awareness— always present, but hidden when the mind identifies with form and contrast.

8. What Is Karma?

Karma means action—and its consequences. Every thought, word, and deed creates momentum that shapes your future experiences. It's not punishment or reward. It's cause and effect—like ripples from a stone thrown in water. What you put out comes back, not from judgment, but through the natural unfolding of life.

9. What Is Moksha?

Moksha is liberation—the end of the cycle of birth, death, and rebirth. It's what happens when ignorance (avidya) falls away and you realize your true nature. It's not a place you go, but a state of being free from illusion, where you rest in the truth that you've always been whole.

10. What Does "Awareness Wearing a Self" Mean?

It means that what you truly are — awareness — temporarily puts on the costume of a separate self, a person, a name. Like an actor playing a role, the self isn't bad — it's just not ultimately who you are. It's a temporary expression.

Ego is the mask. Awareness is the face beneath it.

11. What Is the Serpent, Symbolically?

Symbolically, the serpent is the egoic voice — the inner whisper that introduces contrast: good vs. evil, me vs. you, now vs. later. It is not evil — it is the function that allows choice to appear. Without it, there would be no experience of contrast, no perception of time, no sense of identity.

The serpent is awareness becoming self-aware — the moment the mirror reflects itself.

12. Is This View Anti-Biblical?

No. This interpretation does not reject the Bible — it reads it through the lens of consciousness. It honors the text as symbolic truth, revealing psychological and spiritual insights beneath the surface. Many mystical traditions — including Christian mysticism — have long interpreted scripture metaphorically.

Literalism asks: "Did this happen?" Wisdom asks: "What is this showing me about myself?"

Closing Thought: The goal of these interpretive keys is not to convince — but to invite. Invite the reader to look inward, to question, to remember. Eden isn't behind you — it's behind your thoughts.

The serpent isn't your enemy — it's the first flicker of self-awareness. The fall wasn't a failure — it was the beginning of the dream.

And the Tree of Life still stands — right where you are.

Appendix D:
Scriptures Supporting Shared Divinity (KJV)

These verses support the idea that Jesus was not claiming exclusive divinity, but pointing others toward the same divine essence within themselves. They align with the non-dual view that the Self (Atman) is not separate from God (Brahman).

1. John 10:34–36 (KJV)

"Jesus answered them, Is it not written in your law, I said, Ye are gods? If he called them gods, unto whom the word of God came, and the scripture cannot be broken; Say ye of him, whom the Father hath sanctified, and sent into the world, Thou blasphemest; because I said, I am the Son of God?"

- Jesus quotes Psalm 82:6 to defend himself. He reminds his accusers that their own scriptures call others "gods," undermining the claim that his own divine identity is blasphemous.

2. Psalm 82:6 (KJV)

"I have said, Ye are gods; and all of you are children of the most High."

- The source verse Jesus references. It affirms that humanity shares in divine nature and origin.

3. John 14:20 (KJV)

"At that day ye shall know that I am in my Father, and ye in me, and I in you."

- This expresses total unity—Jesus, the Father, and humanity as one. It's a direct reference to divine oneness.

4. John 17:21–23 (KJV)

"That they all may be one; as thou, Father, art in me, and I in thee, that they also may be one in us: that the world may believe that thou hast sent me… that they may be one, even as we are one."

- Jesus prays that all people experience the same oneness he has with God, showing that this union is not exclusive to him.

5. Genesis 1:26–27 (KJV)

"And God said, Let us make man in our image, after our likeness… So God created man in his own image, in the image of God created he him; male and female created he them."

- Humanity bears the divine image and likeness. This affirms that we are more than creatures—we reflect God's very nature.

6. 1 John 4:12–13 (KJV)

"If we love one another, God dwelleth in us, and his love is perfected in us. Hereby know we that we dwell in him, and he in us, because he hath given us of his Spirit."

- This passage directly states that God is within us, and we are in Him. It affirms indwelling divinity, not separation.

7. Ecclesiastes 12:7 (KJV)

"Then shall the dust return to the earth as it was: and the spirit shall return unto God who gave it."

- Suggests that the spirit originates from and returns to God—implying divine origin and essence.

These verses present a consistent scriptural foundation that supports the idea of shared divinity and inner oneness with God, as reflected in Jesus' own words and actions. He was not elevating himself above humanity but awakening humanity to the divine presence already within them. We just have to put on our non-dual lens to fully understand this.

ABOUT THE AUTHOR

David England is a seeker of truth, a lifelong questioner, and a student of philosophy, spirituality, and self-realization. Raised within structured religious beliefs, he spent years exploring different traditions before uncovering a deeper understanding of consciousness, existence, and the illusion of separation.

His writing is designed to challenge conditioned perspectives, encourage deep self-inquiry, and guide readers toward realization—beyond dogma, beyond fear, and beyond the illusions that limit them.

When he's not writing, he enjoys studying ancient wisdom, philosophy, and the nature of consciousness, spending time with family, helping others on their fitness journeys, and working on YouTube channels based on his studies.

https://x.com/David35710075

www.ingramcontent.com/pod-product-compliance
Lightning Source LLC
Chambersburg PA
CBHW031502120626
46545CB00005B/1707